THE
SHAKESPEARE
HAGGADAH

ELEVATE THY SEDER
WITH THE BARD OF AVON

MARTIN BODEK

WICKED SON

A WICKED SON BOOK
An Imprint of Post Hill Press
ISBN: 978-1-63758-938-0
ISBN (eBook): 978-1-63758-623-5

The Shakespeare Haggadah:
Elevate Thy Seder with the Bard of Avon
© 2023 by Martin M. Bodek
All Rights Reserved

Cover design by Cody Corcoran
Interior Design by Yoni Limor, www.YoniLimor.com

This book tis based on works of fiction, and some tis based on works of historical fiction. The characters, incidents, and dialogues art not products of the author's imagination. Rather, these art the products of the imagination of one William Shakespeare, from Stratford-upon-Avon in England, to which the author hath applied homage via parody. These works hast now been part of the public domain for centuries. If it be true thou hast copyright issues with this book, wend complain to William's grave, whither a curse awaits thee. Hast excitement.

Post Hill Press
New York • Nashville
wickedsonbooks.com
posthillpress.com

Published in the United States of America
1 2 3 4 5 6 7 8 9 10

---

1   Hamlet, Act 1, Scene 3.

For Chanalah

Peace, here comes my sister, reading.[2]

As You Like It, Act 3, Scene 2.

Of Such Contents as You Will Wonder At[3]

---

3   *The Merry Wives of Windsor*, Act 4, Scene 6.

ACT III

ACT IV

ACT V

To Be Acknowledged[4]

Effects of courtesy, dues of gratitude.[5] Heaven, set ope thy everlasting gates, to entertain my vows of thanks and praise.[6]

O Lord, that lends me life, Lend me a heart replete with thankfulness! For Thou hast given me in this beauteous face a world of earthly blessings to my soul.[7] I thank God I have been so well brought up that I can write my name.[8]

My queen, my wife, my life, O Naomi, Naomi, Naomi.[9]

Mine eldest daughter and my joy,[10] Naava.

My eldest son, Lord Freddy, whose virtues will, I hope, reflect as Titan's rays on earth, and ripen justice in this commonweal.[11]

My youngest son, Ranan, a true knight. Not yet mature, yet matchless. Firm of word, speaking in deeds.[12]

The most noble mother of the world,[13] Chantze.

My Aba, Chaim, you are my father too and did relieve me, to see this gracious season.[14]

My father Barry's love is enough to honour him enough.[15]

To my mum, Lea, I give thanks in part of thy deserts, and will with deeds requite thy gentleness.[16]

I have a kind soul that would give my mother-in-law Rochelle thanks and knows not how to do it but with tears.[17]

Be to thy person, noble father-in-law, Leon. Fortune and victory sit on thy helm.[18]

---

4   *The Winter's Tale,* Act 4, Scene 4.
5   *King Lear,* Act 2, Scene 4.
6   *Henry VI, Part II,* Act 4, Scene 9.
7   *Ibid,* Act 1, Scene 1.
8   *Ibid,* Act 4, Scene 2.
9   *Cymbeline,* Act 5, Scene 5.
10   *Henry VI, Part III,* Act 3, Scene 3.
11   *Titus Andronicus,* Act 1, Scene 1.
12   *Troilus and Cressida,* Act 4, Scene 5.
13   *Coriolanus,* Act 5, Scene 3.
14   *Cymbeline,* Act 5, Scene 5.
15   *As You Like It,* Act 1, Scene 2.
16   *Titus Andronicus,* Act 1, Scene 1.
17   *King John,* Act 5, Scene 7.
18   *Richard III,* Act 5, Scene 3.

Michael Szpilzinger, Doodie Miller, Darryl Singh, Stephen Schwartz, Chesky Rand, Ditza Katz, Ross Tabisel, Rav Pinky Schmeckelstein, Shia Itzkowitz, Sandy Eller, Eli Friedman, Shai Grabie, Jamey Kohn, Marc H. Simon, Shloime Drillick, Rabbi Mordechai Finkelman, Binyamin Jolkovsky, Danny Levine, Tzvi Mauer, Moshe Kinderlehrer, Alon Stempel, Sandy Eller, Dina Vinar-Cieplinski, Jodi Goldberg, Shia Itzkowitz, Avi Lew, Malky Tannenbaum Haimoff, Meir Kruter, Chaim Howard Nath, Dan Shuman, Michael Szpilzinger, Viva La Jewpacabra, Mitchell Silk, Chanan Feldman, Joel Mandel, Moshe Lewis, Rachel Warshower, Azi Steiner, David Schlachter, Avi Koplowitz, Shmuly Engelman, Ari Benscher, Benjamin Lieberman, Adam Orlow, Peretz Stern, Chezky Rosenblum, Matt Katz, Steven Friedman, Steven Holmbraker, Yaakov Bressler, Kfir Ovadia, Bentzi Gruber, Yeedle Licthenstein, Naftali Lichtenstein, Devorah Wicentowsky, Sara Shuman, Benzion Werczberger, Efraim Bloch, my fifteen Malik cousins and their spouses and their children, Reb Aharon Zev Malik, Laizer Moshe Malik, thanks, gentle citizens and friends, quoth I, this general applause and loving shout argues your wisdoms and your loves.[19]

For your many courtesies, I thank you, Mordechai and Tova Ovits.[20]

David Adler, I can nothing render but allegiant thanks. My prayers to heaven for you, my loyalty, which ever has and ever shall be growing, till death, that winter kill it.[21]

Yaakov Sash, my life itself, and the best heart of it, thank you.[22]

Uncle Michael, Omi Sue, Aron, Ilana, Eytan, Chaya, Aliza, Simon, Joel, and Avital Storfer. Uncle Sooty, Auntie Hazel, Benjy, Laura, Jeremy, Jess, David, and Jonathan Israel. Are they not but in Britain?[23] To mingle friendship far is mingling bloods.[24]

Anna Olswanger, Marnie Winston-MacAuley, Rabbi Cary Friedman, Mark Levinson, Jonathan Tropper, David Bader, Joel Chasnoff, Jon Stewart, Lisa Alcalay Klug, Algonquin Jones, A.J. Jacobs, Sam Reinstein, Dave Cowen, you great benefactors, sprinkle our society with thankfulness. For your own gifts, make yourselves praised.[25] A thousand thanks.[26]

---

19   *Ibid*, Act 3, Scene 7.
20   *Much Ado About Nothing*, Act 5, Scene 1.
21   *Henry VIII*, Act 3, Scene 2.
22   *Ibid*, Act 1, Scene 2.
23   *Cymbeline*, Act 3, Scene 4.
24   *The Winter's Tale*, Act 3, Scene 2.
25   *Timon of Athens*, Act 3, Scene 6.
26   *Henry V*, Act 4, Scene 4.

And so I thank you for your good counsel,[27] my hockey guys, Yaakov Ochs, Meir Kruter, Mo Sanders, Baal Habos, Shia Itzkowitz, Sruli Derdik, Sandy Eller, Marnie Winston-MacAuley, Yossie Davis, Dov Kramer, Michal Alatin, Chanalah Bodek, Chaiy Bodek, Sarra Laskin, Bekka Laskin, Bettina Laskin, Steve Lipman, Josh Weinstein, Niko Pfund, Nancy Toff, Deborah Shor, Ada Brunstein, and Susan Ferber.

Dena Szpilzinger, Yiddy Lebovits, Elizabeth Ehrenpreis, in framing an artist, art hath thus decreed, to make some good, but others to exceed.[28]

Jeff Goodstein, only I have left to say, more is thy due than more than all can pay.[29]

Moishey Sharf, well then, if ever I thank any man, I'll thank you.[30]

I can no other answer make but thanks, and thanks, and ever thanks.[31]

---

27   *Hamlet*, Act 4, Scene 5.
28   *Pericles*, Act 2, Scene 3.
29   *Macbeth*, Act 1, Scene 4.
30   *As You Like It*, Act 2, Scene 5.
31   *Twelfth Night*, Act 3, Scene 3.

The Prologue Is Addressed[32]

This is mine tenth book and mine fourth Haggadah. Not did I design it thus—Purim is mine highest in estimation Jewish festival, for I share a Hebrew name with the protagonist—but something wicked this way[33] clicked after I published *The Emoji Haggadah*.

Usually, after I conclude a thing of grandeur, mine wife asketh, "What be next for thee, mine handsome husband?" The answer in that instance turned out wast *The Festivus Haggadah*.

Then a certain pandemic toldeth what's next ere mine wife could coequal asketh again. *The Coronavirus Haggadah* wast born.

Suddenly I wast the author of three haggadot, so what be next again? Turns out, a certain comedic author named Dave Cowen hadst been cranking out haggadot himself, and we wast be-tied. I now needed to pull ahead, because I'm going for the Guinness record, if it be true in fact, I don't already own it. I should check.

I pondered all of pop culture options, and settled on the one idea that a. might not receiveth me sued for copyright infringement, b. is timeless, eternal, popular, and c. I would hast lots of fun with because I'm a fan myself. Bingo. *The Shakespeare Haggadah*.

I laid down several goals and ground rules to increase mine own fun and the enjoyment of the reader:

1. I wished to finally maketh a haggadah with maximum utility, so for the first time, I would maketh a parody haggadah with the Hebrew facing text. Bam.

2. I wished to weave as many of Shakespeare' famous, and non-famous, quotes into the narrative, wherever relevant. Bazinga. 433 quotation footnotes, for thy reading pleasure.

---

32 *A Midsummer Night's Dream*, Act 5, Scene 1.
33 *Macbeth*, Act 4, Scene 1.

3. I wished at least one footnote per translated page. If it be true I couldst not meeteth that minimum, I wast not working hard enough.

4. I wished to quoteth every single one of The Bard's plays, multiple times. Baboom!, every play is quoted a minimum of five times.

I completed the book on Festivus Eve, ironically, and am quite pleased with the final product. Cowen is working on something, but I'veth pulled ahead. I shall contacteth Guinness whilst thou hast a joyous Passover.

The Shakespeare Haggadah

—

ACT I

The bare-picked
bone of majesty[34]

Roasted egg in wrath and fire[35]   Withered herbs[36]

Parsley to stuff a rabbit[37]   Lump of clay[38]

The enchanted herbs[39]

---

34   *King John*, Act 4, Scene 3.
35   *Hamlet*, Act 2, Scene 2.
36   *Titus Andronicus*, Act 3, Scene 1.
37   *The Taming of the Shrew*, Act 4, Scene 4.
38   *Henry VI*, Part I, Act 2, Scene 5.
39   *The Merchant of Venice*, Act 5, Scene 1.

קַדֵּשׁ

[הבעל נכנס, בעקבות בית הכנסת. הוא מלביש הקיטל הלבן שלו, שכבר
יש בו כתמי מיץ ענבים משום מה. האישה היפה מוטרדת, כועסת שבעלה איחר.
ארבעת הבנים מתקוטטים. המחותנים שקטים, לפי ההזמנה. האורחים תוהים מה
מחכה להם.]

מוזגים כוס ראשון. המצות מכוסות.

קַדֵּשׁ

בְּשַׁבָּת מַתְחִילִין:

וַיְהִי עֶרֶב וַיְהִי בֹקֶר יוֹם הַשִּׁשִּׁי. וַיְכֻלּוּ הַשָּׁמַיִם
וְהָאָרֶץ וְכָל־צְבָאָם. וַיְכַל אֱלֹהִים בַּיּוֹם הַשְּׁבִיעִי
מְלַאכְתּוֹ אֲשֶׁר עָשָׂה וַיִּשְׁבֹּת בַּיּוֹם הַשְּׁבִיעִי מִכָּל
מְלַאכְתּוֹ אֲשֶׁר עָשָׂה. וַיְבָרֶךְ אֱלֹהִים אֶת יוֹם
הַשְּׁבִיעִי וַיְקַדֵּשׁ אוֹתוֹ כִּי בוֹ שָׁבַת מִכָּל־.מְלַאכְתּוֹ
אֲשֶׁר בָּרָא אֱלֹהִים לַעֲשׂוֹת׳.

Sanctification

[The husband enters, following synagogue. He dons his thin white robe, which already has grape juice stains for some reason. The wife is harried, beautiful, upset her husband is late. The four sons are squabbling. The in-laws are quiet, as ordered. The guests wonder what's in store.]

We poureth the first cup of wine, that's brisk and fine.[40] *The unleavened halfpennyworth of breads*[41] *art covered.*

Speaketh the sanctification speech, trippingly on the tongue.[42]

And by our holy Sabbath,[43] *beginneth hither:*

And thither wast evening and thither wast morning's face,[44] the sixth day. And the heaven and the earth wast finished, and O all you host.[45] And on the seventh day God finished His love's labour[46] which He hadst done and He did rest the innocent sleep[47] on the seventh day from all His love's labour which He hadst done. And God did bless the seventh day and did sanctify it because He did rest on sleep that knits up the raveled sleave of care[48] from all of His love's labour which God did create in doing.

---

40   *Henry IV*, Part II, Act 5, Scene 3.

41   *Henry IV*, Part I, Act 2, Scene 4.

42   *Hamlet*, Act 3, Scene 2.

43   *The Merchant of Venice*, Act 4, Scene 1.

44   *Romeo and Juliet*, Act 4, Scene 5.

45   *Hamlet*, Act 1, Scene 5.

46   Too easy.

47   *Macbeth*, Act 2, Scene 2.

48   *Ibid.*

סַבְרִי מָרָנָן וְרַבָּנָן וְרַבּוֹתַי. בָּרוּךְ אַתָּה ה אֱלֹהֵינוּ מֶלֶךְ הָעוֹלָם בּוֹרֵא פְּרִי הַגָּפֶן.

בָּרוּךְ אַתָּה ה', אֱלֹהֵינוּ מֶלֶךְ הָעוֹלָם אֲשֶׁר בָּחַר בָּנוּ מִכָּל־עָם וְרוֹמְמָנוּ מִכָּל־לָשׁוֹן וְקִדְּשָׁנוּ בְּמִצְוֹתָיו. וַתִּתֶּן לָנוּ ה' אֱלֹהֵינוּ בְּאַהֲבָה (לשבת: שַׁבָּתוֹת לִמְנוּחָה וּ) מוֹעֲדִים לְשִׂמְחָה, חַגִּים וּזְמַנִּים לְשָׂשׂוֹן, (לשבת: אֶת יוֹם הַשַּׁבָּת הַזֶּה וְ) אֶת יוֹם חַג הַמַּצּוֹת הַזֶּה זְמַן חֵרוּתֵנוּ, (לשבת: בְּאַהֲבָה) מִקְרָא קֹדֶשׁ זֵכֶר לִיצִיאַת מִצְרָיִם. כִּי בָנוּ בָחַרְתָּ וְאוֹתָנוּ קִדַּשְׁתָּ מִכָּל הָעַמִּים, (לשבת: וְשַׁבָּת) וּמוֹעֲדֵי קָדְשֶׁךָ (לשבת: בְּאַהֲבָה וּבְרָצוֹן) בְּשִׂמְחָה וּבְשָׂשׂוֹן הִנְחַלְתָּנוּ.

בָּרוּךְ אַתָּה ה', מְקַדֵּשׁ (לשבת: הַשַּׁבָּת וְ) יִשְׂרָאֵל וְהַזְּמַנִּים.

On weekdays, beginneth hither:

Friends, Romans, countrymen, lend me your ears.[49]
Blessed art Thee now, Lord our God be praised,[50]
king of the universe, who maketh the fruit of the
vine, the merry cheerer of the heart.[51]

Blessed art thee, Lord our God, our fortress,[52]
king of the wide vessel of the universe,[53] who
hath chosen us from all peoples and hath raised us
above all tongues and hath sanctified us with His
commandments. And thou hast given us, Lord our
God, sabbaths for rest, appointed times for happiness, holidays, and special times for this, general
joy,[54] this sabbath day, and] this festival of leavened breads, our season of freedom in love a holy
convocation in memory of the unpeopling[55] from
Egypt. For Thou hast chosen us and sanctified
us above all peoples. In thy gracious love, Thee
granted us Thy holy sabbath, and special times for
happiness and joy.

Blessed art thee, O Lord, Sir[56] who sanctifies (the
Sabbath), Israel, and the appointed times.

---

49   *Julius Caesar*, Act 3, Scene 2.

50   *Henry VI*, Act 2, Scene 1.

51   *Henry V*, Act 5, Scene 2.

52   *Henry VI, Part I*, Act 2, Scene 1.

53   *Henry V*, Act 4, Chorus.

54   *Henry VIII*, Act 4, Scene 1.

55   *Antony and Cleopatra*, Act I, Scene 5.

56   *All's Well That Ends Well*, Act 2 Scene 2.

בָּרוּךְ אַתָּה ה', אֱלֹהֵינוּ מֶלֶךְ הָעוֹלָם, בּוֹרֵא מְאוֹרֵי
הָאֵשׁ. בָּרוּךְ אַתָּה ה', אֱלֹהֵינוּ מֶלֶךְ הָעוֹלָם הַמַּבְדִּיל
בֵּין קֹדֶשׁ לְחֹל, בֵּין אוֹר לְחֹשֶׁךְ, בֵּין יִשְׂרָאֵל
לָעַמִּים, בֵּין יוֹם הַשְּׁבִיעִי לְשֵׁשֶׁת יְמֵי הַמַּעֲשֶׂה. בֵּין
קְדֻשַּׁת שַׁבָּת לִקְדֻשַּׁת יוֹם טוֹב הִבְדַּלְתָּ, וְאֶת־יוֹם
הַשְּׁבִיעִי מִשֵּׁשֶׁת יְמֵי הַמַּעֲשֶׂה קִדַּשְׁתָּ. הִבְדַּלְתָּ
וְקִדַּשְׁתָּ אֶת־עַמְּךָ יִשְׂרָאֵל בִּקְדֻשָּׁתֶךָ.

בָּרוּךְ אַתָּה ה', הַמַּבְדִּיל בֵּין קֹדֶשׁ לְקֹדֶשׁ.

On Saturday night addeth the following two paragraphs:

Blessed art thee, Lord our God, hail, great King[57] of the universe, who maketh the light of the fire. Blessed art thee, Lord our God, King of the universe, who distinguishes betwixt[58] the holy and the profane, betwixt light and utter darkness,[59] betwixt Israel and the nations, between the seventh day and the six working days, for which we are but warriors.[60] Thou hast distinguished betwixt the holiness of the Sabbath and the holiness of all things that we ordained Festival,[61] and thou hast sanctified the seventh day above the six working days. thou hast distinguished and sanctified thy people Israel with thy holiness.

Blessed art thee, O Lord, good my Lord captain,[62] who distinguishes betwixt the holy and the holy.

---

57   *Cymbeline*, Act 5, Scene 5.

58   *Othello*, Act 1, Scene 3.

59   *Henry IV*, Part 1, Scene 3, Act 3.

60   *Henry V*, Act 4, Scene 3.

61   *Romeo and Juliet*, Act 4, Scene 5.

62   *Henry IV*, Part II, Act 3, Scene 2.

בָּרוּךְ אַתָּה ה', אֱלֹהֵינוּ מֶלֶךְ הָעוֹלָם, שֶׁהֶחֱיָנוּ
וְקִיְּמָנוּ וְהִגִּיעָנוּ לַזְּמַן הַזֶּה.

שותה בהסיבת שמאל ואינו מברך ברכה אחרונה.

[כתמים טריים נמצאים כעת על קיטל הבעל, אבל הפעם הסיבה הייתה
ברורה. הוא קצת יותר מדי בעניין. אין לו חילוף. האישה מגלגלת את עיניה.
כולם מתיישבים עכשיו ליד השולחן.]

22

Blessed art thee, O Lord, our God, the King for all the world,[63] who hath given life to us and established us by the consent of all[64] and hath made us cometh to this time.

Drinketh while reclining to the left and doth not recite a blessing after drinking.

[*Fresh stains are now on the husband's robe, but this time the reason was obvious. He's a little too into it. He has no spare. The wife rolls her eyes. Everyone now takes their seat at the table.*]

---

63   *Henry VIII*, Act 2, Scene 3.
64   *Coriolanus*, Act 3, Scene 1.

וּרְחַץ

[כיור וספל מים מובא על ידי ילד צייתן לבעל, שהוא - כן, בהחלט. הוא הולך למטבח בעצמו בזמן שהבנים מתכננים מראש את מיקוח האפיקומן עם האישה. הבעל יוצא.]

נוטלים את הידים ואין מברכים "עַל נְטִילַת יָדָיִם."

[הבעל חוזר.]

24

And Washeth and Welcome Heartily[65]

[*A washbasin is brought by an obedient member of the family to the husband who—yeah, right, he traipses off to the kitchen himself while the sons pre-plan the afikoman bargaining with the wife. The husband exits.*]

It will please thy mightiness to wash thy hands[66] but doth not say the blessing "on the washing of the hands."

[*The husband returns.*]

---

65   *The Taming of the Shrew*, Act 4, Scene 1.
66   *Ibid*, Prologue.

כַּרְפַּס

[הבעל רחץ ידיים כדי שיוכל לחלק את הירוקים לכולם. זו התקופה
היחידה בשנה שהבעל מבצע את החובה הזו. השרוולים שלו תופסים הכל.
האישה מגלגלת את עיניה. המחותנים עדיין, איכשהו, סותמים את הפה שלהם.
השפתיים של האורחים עדיין רוכסות.]

לוקח מן הכרפס פחות מכזית – כדי שלא יתחייב בברכה אחרונה –
טובל במי מלח, מברך "בורא פרי האדמה", ומכוין לפטור בברכה
גם את המרור. אוכל בלא הסבה.

בָּרוּךְ אַתָּה ה', אֱלֹהֵינוּ מֶלֶךְ הָעוֹלָם, בּוֹרֵא פְּרִי
הָאֲדָמָה.

March These Greens[67]

[The husband washed his hands so that he could apportion the greens to everyone. This is the only time of year the husband performs this duty. His sleeves catch everything. The wife rolls her eyes. The in-laws still, somehow, keep their mouths shut. The lips of the guests are still zipped.]

Taketh from the sea-water greens, sir,[68] less than an olive's measure so that thee wilt not needeth to sayeth the blessing after eating it, dippeth it into the saltwater, sayeth the blessing "who maketh the fruit of the earth" and hast in mind that this blessing wilt beest for the bitter herbs. consumeth without reclining.

Blessed art thee, Lord our God, King of the universe, who maketh the fruit of the earth.

---

67   *King John*, Act 2, Scene 1.
68   *Love's Labour's Lost*, Act 1, Scene 2.

יַחַץ

חותך את המצה האמצעית לשתים, ומצפין את הנתח הגדול לאפיקומן.

[הבעל מניח את החתיכה הגדולה יותר בתוך שקית אפיקומן קטן וחמוד שהקטן יצר, ומסתיר אותה מאחורי גבו כי אף אחד לא ימצא את זה שם.]

28

Suddenly Break Forth[69]

We split, we split, we split[70] the middle unleavened bread in two, and concealeth the larger piece to useth it for the dessert between our after-supper and bedtime.[71]

[The husband places the larger piece in a cute little sash that the little one created and hides it behind his back because nobody is on to him.]

---

69   *As You Like It,* Act I, Scene 2.

70   *The Tempest,* Act 2, Scene I.

71   *A Midsummer Night's Dream,* Act 5, Scene I.

מַגִּיד

Telling of Discreet Stories[72]

—

ACT II

הָא לַחְמָא עַנְיָא

מגלה את המצות, מגביה את הקערה ואומר בקול רם:

הָא לַחְמָא עַנְיָא דִּי אֲכָלוּ אַבְהָתָנָא בְּאַרְעָא
דְמִצְרָיִם. כָּל דִּכְפִין יֵיתֵי וְיֵיכֹל, כָּל דִּצְרִיךְ יֵיתֵי
וְיִפְסַח. הָשַׁתָּא הָכָא, לְשָׁנָה הַבָּאָה בְּאַרְעָא
דְיִשְׂרָאֵל. הָשַׁתָּא עַבְדֵי, לְשָׁנָה הַבָּאָה בְּנֵי חוֹרִין.

This Is the Bitter Bread of Banishment[73]

The vaward uncovers the unleavened breads, raiseth the Seder plate, and sayeth out loud:

This is the bitter bread of banishment that our ancestors consumed in the land of Egypt. Anyone who is filthy famished[74] should cometh and consumeth, anyone who is in need should cometh and by and by thy bosom shall partake[75] of the Passover sacrifice. Now we art hither, next year we wilt beest in the land of Israel. This year we art slaves, next year we wilt beest free people.

73   *Richard II*, Act 3, Scene 1.
74   *Henry IV*, Part II, Act 5, Scene 4.
75   *Julius Caesar*, Act 2, Scene 1.

מַה נִּשְׁתַּנָּה

מסיר את הקערה מעל השולחן. מוזגין כוס שני. הבן שואל:

[הבן הצעיר מסרב לשאול, אז הצעיר הבא מוזמן לדקלם את השאלות.
הוויכוחים נמשכים, עד שאיכשהו, האדם המבוגר ביותר בשולחן עושה זאת
בסופו של דבר.]

מַה נִּשְׁתַּנָּה הַלַּיְלָה הַזֶּה מִכָּל הַלֵּילוֹת? שֶׁבְּכָל
הַלֵּילוֹת אָנוּ אוֹכְלִין חָמֵץ וּמַצָּה, הַלַּיְלָה הַזֶּה – כֻּלּוֹ
מַצָּה. שֶׁבְּכָל הַלֵּילוֹת אָנוּ אוֹכְלִין שְׁאָר יְרָקוֹת –
הַלַּיְלָה הַזֶּה (כֻּלּוֹ) מָרוֹר. שֶׁבְּכָל הַלֵּילוֹת אֵין אָנוּ
מַטְבִּילִין אֲפִילוּ פַּעַם אֶחָת – הַלַּיְלָה הַזֶּה שְׁתֵּי
פְעָמִים. שֶׁבְּכָל הַלֵּילוֹת אָנוּ אוֹכְלִין בֵּין יוֹשְׁבִין
וּבֵין מְסֻבִּין – הַלַּיְלָה הַזֶּה כֻּלָּנוּ מְסֻבִּין.

34

The Four Questions

He removeth the plate from the table. We poureth a second cup of wine. The son then asketh:

> [*The youngest son refuses to ask, so the next youngest is bidden to recite the questions. The arguing continues, until, somehow, the oldest person at the table ends up doing it.*]

What differentiates this night from all [other] nights? On all [other] nights we consumeth leavened breads and unleavened breads; this night, only unleavened breads. On all [other] nights we consumeth other vegetables; tonight we only chew the food of sweet and bitter fancy.[76] On all other nights, we doth not dippeth our food, coequal one time; tonight we dippeth it twice. On all] other nights, we consumeth either sitting or reclining; tonight we all reclineth.

---

76   *As You Like It*, Act 4, Scene 3.

עֲבָדִים הָיִינוּ לְפַרְעֹה בְּמִצְרַיִם

מחזיר את הקערה אל השולחן. המצות תהיינה מגלות בשעת
אמירת ההגדה.

[הבעל מתחיל בקריאה שלו ולפתע מתפוצצת סביבו השיחה. הוא
ממשיך, וככל הנראה, כל השאר יצטרפו לחלקים המהנים.]

עֲבָדִים הָיִינוּ לְפַרְעֹה בְּמִצְרַיִם, וַיּוֹצִיאֵנוּ ה' אֱלֹהֵינוּ
מִשָּׁם בְּיָד חֲזָקָה וּבִזְרֹעַ נְטוּיָה. וְאִלּוּ לֹא הוֹצִיא
הַקָּדוֹשׁ בָּרוּךְ הוּא אֶת אֲבוֹתֵינוּ מִמִּצְרַיִם, הֲרֵי אָנוּ
וּבָנֵינוּ וּבְנֵי בָנֵינוּ מְשֻׁעְבָּדִים הָיִינוּ לְפַרְעֹה
בְּמִצְרָיִם. וַאֲפִילוּ כֻּלָּנוּ חֲכָמִים כֻּלָּנוּ נְבוֹנִים כֻּלָּנוּ
זְקֵנִים כֻּלָּנוּ יוֹדְעִים אֶת הַתּוֹרָה מִצְוָה עָלֵינוּ לְסַפֵּר
בִּיצִיאַת מִצְרָיִם. וְכָל הַמַּרְבֶּה לְסַפֵּר בִּיצִיאַת
מִצְרַיִם הֲרֵי זֶה מְשֻׁבָּח.

We Wast Slaves in Egypt

He putteth the plate back on the table. The unleavened breads should beest uncovered during the saying of the Haggadah.

[The husband begins his recitation and suddenly conversation explodes around him. He motors along, and presumably, everyone else will join in for the fun parts.]

We wast slaves to Pharaoh in the land of Egypt. And the Lord, our God, tooketh us out from there but to recover of us with a strong hand[77] and an outstretched forearm. And if the Holy One, blessed be He, had not taken our ancestors from Egypt, behold we and our children and our children's children would [all] be enslaved to Pharaoh in Egypt. And even if were all you sage counsellors,[78] all in thy brows an eye discerning,[79] all most reverend and grave elders,[80] all knowledgeable about the Torah, it would be a commandment upon us to tell the story of the exodus from Egypt. And anyone who adds and spendeth extra time] in telling the story of the exodus from Egypt, behold thou art to praise, thy praise's worth.[81]

---

77   *Hamlet*, Act 1, Scene 1.
78   *Henry IV*, Part II, Act 4, Scene 5.
79   *King Lear*, Act 4, Scene 2.
80   *Coriolanus*, Act 2, Scene 2.
81   *King Edward III*, Act 2, Scene 1.

סִיפּוּר שֶׁל הַחֲמִשָּׁה רַבָּנִים

מַעֲשֶׂה בְּרַבִּי אֱלִיעֶזֶר וְרַבִּי יְהוֹשֻׁעַ וְרַבִּי אֶלְעָזָר
בֶּן־עֲזַרְיָה וְרַבִּי עֲקִיבָא וְרַבִּי טַרְפוֹן שֶׁהָיוּ מְסֻבִּין
בִּבְנֵי־בְרַק וְהָיוּ מְסַפְּרִים בִּיצִיאַת מִצְרַיִם כָּל־אוֹתוֹ
הַלַּיְלָה, עַד שֶׁבָּאוּ תַלְמִידֵיהֶם וְאָמְרוּ לָהֶם רַבּוֹתֵינוּ
הִגִּיעַ זְמַן קְרִיאַת שְׁמַע שֶׁל שַׁחֲרִית.

אָמַר רַבִּי אֶלְעָזָר בֶּן־עֲזַרְיָה הֲרֵי אֲנִי כְּבֶן שִׁבְעִים
שָׁנָה וְלֹא זָכִיתִי שֶׁתֵּאָמֵר יְצִיאַת מִצְרַיִם בַּלֵּילוֹת
עַד שֶׁדְּרָשָׁהּ בֶּן זוֹמָא, שֶׁנֶּאֱמַר[ii], לְמַעַן תִּזְכֹּר אֶת
יוֹם צֵאתְךָ מֵאֶרֶץ מִצְרַיִם כֹּל יְמֵי חַיֶּיךָ. יְמֵי חַיֶּיךָ
הַיָּמִים. כֹּל יְמֵי חַיֶּיךָ הַלֵּילוֹת. וַחֲכָמִים אוֹמְרִים יְמֵי
חַיֶּיךָ הָעוֹלָם הַזֶּה. כֹּל יְמֵי חַיֶּיךָ לְהָבִיא לִימוֹת
הַמָּשִׁיחַ.

[ii] Deuteronomy 16:3.

Story of the Five Holy Clergymen[82]

It hath happened once on Passover that Clergyman Eliezer, Clergyman Yehoshua, Clergyman Elazar ben Azariah, Clergyman Akiva and Clergyman Tarfon wast reclining in Bnei Brak and wast telling the story of the exodus from Egypt up this hour awake all night,[83] until their students cameth and said to them, "The time of [reciting] the morning Shema hath arrived."

Clergyman Elazar ben Azariah said, "Behold I had rather, forsooth, go before thee like a man[84] of seventy years and I have not merited [to understand why] the exodus from Egypt should be said at night until Ben Zoma explicated it, as it is stated, 'In order that you remember the day of your going out from the land of Egypt all the days of your life;' 'the days of your life indicates that the remembrance be invoked during] the days, 'all the days of your life' indicates that the remembrance be invoked also during] the nights." But the Sages say, "the days of your life 'indicates that the remembrance be invoked in this world, *all* the days of your life' indicates that the remembrance be invoked also in the days of the Messiah."

---

82   *Richard II*, Act 4, Scene 1.
83   *Julius Caesar*, Act 2, Scene 1.
84   *The Merry Wives of Windsor*, Act 3, Scene 2.

אַרְבָּעָה בָנִים

בָּרוּךְ הַמָּקוֹם, בָּרוּךְ הוּא, בָּרוּךְ שֶׁנָּתַן תּוֹרָה לְעַמּוֹ יִשְׂרָאֵל, בָּרוּךְ הוּא. כְּנֶגֶד אַרְבָּעָה בָנִים דִּבְּרָה תוֹרָה: אֶחָד חָכָם, וְאֶחָד רָשָׁע, וְאֶחָד תָּם, וְאֶחָד שֶׁאֵינוֹ יוֹדֵעַ לִשְׁאוֹל.

חָכָם מָה הוּא אוֹמֵר? מָה הָעֵדוֹת וְהַחֻקִּים וְהַמִּשְׁפָּטִים אֲשֶׁר צִוָּה ה' אֱלֹהֵינוּ אֶתְכֶם.iii וְאַף אַתָּה אֱמֹר לוֹ כְּהִלְכוֹת הַפֶּסַח: אֵין מַפְטִירִין אַחַר הַפֶּסַח אֲפִיקוֹמָן.iv

רָשָׁע מָה הוּא אוֹמֵר? מָה הָעֲבוֹדָה הַזֹּאת לָכֶם.v לָכֶם – וְלֹא לוֹ. וּלְפִי שֶׁהוֹצִיא אֶת עַצְמוֹ מִן הַכְּלָל כָּפַר בְּעִקָּר. וְאַף אַתָּה הַקְהֵה אֶת שִׁנָּיו וֶאֱמֹר לוֹ: "בַּעֲבוּר זֶה עָשָׂה ה' לִי בְּצֵאתִי מִמִּצְרָיִם".vi לִי וְלֹא־לוֹ. אִלּוּ הָיָה שָׁם, לֹא הָיָה נִגְאָל.

iii Deuteronomy 6:20.
iv Mishnah Pesachim 10:8.
v Exodus 12:26.
vi Exodus 13.8

The Four Sons

Blessed beest the lodging of all, blessed beest He, blessed beest the One who gaveth the Torah to His people Israel, blessed beest He. Corresponding to four sons didst the Torah speaketh: one [who he is] wise,[85] one who hath kept an evil diet long,[86] one who is as innocent as grace itself,[87] and one who doth not knoweth what's best to asketh.[88]

What doest the wise son sayeth? "What art these testimonies, statutes, and judgments that the Lord our God commanded thee?" And accordingly thou wilt sayeth to him, as per the laws of the Passover sacrifice, "We may not consume an afikoman, a dessert or other foods eaten after the meal, after [we art finished eating] the Passover sacrifice."

What doest the evil son sayeth? What is this worship to thee? 'To thee' and not 'to him.' And since he excluded himself from the collective, he denied a principle of the good Jewish faith, every dram of it.[89] And accordingly, thou shalt give him bloody teeth[90] and sayeth to him. "'For the sake of this, didst the Lord doeth this for *me* in mine going out of Egypt.' For me and not 'for him.' If it be true that he hadst been thither, he wouldst not have been saved.

---

85   *Romeo and Juliet*, Act 2, Scene 1.
86   *Richard III*, Act 1, Scene 1.
87   *As You Like It*, Act 1, Scene 3.
88   *Cymbeline*, Act 5, Scene 5.
89   *All's Well That Ends Well*, Act 2, Scene 3.
90   *Antony and Cleopatra*, Act 1, Scene 5.

תָּם מָה הוּא אוֹמֵר? מַה זֹּאת?[vii] וְאָמַרְתָּ אֵלָיו
"בְּחֹזֶק יָד הוֹצִיאָנוּ ה' מִמִּצְרַיִם מִבֵּית עֲבָדִים[viii]."

וְשֶׁאֵינוֹ יוֹדֵעַ לִשְׁאוֹל — אַתְּ פְּתַח לוֹ, שֶׁנֶּאֱמַר[ix],
וְהִגַּדְתָּ לְבִנְךָ בַּיּוֹם הַהוּא לֵאמֹר, בַּעֲבוּר זֶה עָשָׂה
ה' לִי בְּצֵאתִי מִמִּצְרָיִם.

[vii] *Exodus* 13:14.
[viii] Ibid.
[ix] *Exodus* 13:8.

What doest the innocent [son] sayeth? What is this?"[91] And thee wilt sayeth to him, "With the strength of limb and policy of mind[92] didst the Lord taketh us out from Egypt, from the house of slaves."

And regarding the one who doeth not knoweth to asketh, thee wilt ope that liberty and common conversation[93] for him. As tis stated, And thee wilt speaketh to thy son on that day saying, for the sake of this, didst the Lord doeth this for me in mine going out of Egypt."

91 *Love's Labour's Lost*, Act 5, Scene 2.

92 *Much Ado About Nothing*, Act 4, Scene 1.

93 *The Two Noble Kinsmen*, Act 2, Scene 1.

יָכוֹל מֵראשׁ חֹדֶשׁ?

[הבנים לא אוהבים איך שהם ציירו, למרות שזה היה מדויק. האישה מנחמת את הילדים בעוד הבעל ממשיך. המחותנים והאורחים סוף סוף זוכים לשוחח ולהכיר אחד את השני.]

יָכוֹל מֵראשׁ חֹדֶשׁ? תַּלְמוּד לוֹמַר בַּיוֹם הַהוּא. אִי בַּיוֹם הַהוּא יָכוֹל מִבְּעוֹד יוֹם? תַּלְמוּד לוֹמַר בַּעֲבוּר זֶה — בַּעֲבוּר זֶה לֹא אָמַרְתִּי, אֶלָּא בְּשָׁעָה שֶׁיֵּשׁ מַצָּה וּמָרוֹר מֻנָּחִים לְפָנֶיךָ.

It Could Beest from the Head of the Month

[The sons don't like how they were caricatured, even though it was accurate. The wife consoles the children while the husband motors on, and the in-laws and guests finally get to chat and get to know each other.]

It could beest from the head of the month (that one would hast to speak, breathe, discuss[94] the Exodus). However, we learneth otherwise, since tis stated, "on that day." If it be true tis (written) "on that day," it could beest from while tis still day (before the night of the fifteenth of Nissan. However) we learneth (otherwise, since) tis stated, "for the sake of this." I didst not sayeth "for the sake of this" except (that it beest observed) at which hour (this) unleavened bread and bitter herb art resting in front of thee (meaning, on the night of the fifteenth).

מִתְּחִלָּה עוֹבְדֵי עֲבוֹדָה זָרָה הָיוּ אֲבוֹתֵינוּ

מִתְּחִלָּה עוֹבְדֵי עֲבוֹדָה זָרָה הָיוּ אֲבוֹתֵינוּ, וְעַכְשָׁיו
קֵרְבָנוּ הַמָּקוֹם לַעֲבֹדָתוֹ, שֶׁנֶּאֱמַר:[x] וַיֹּאמֶר יְהוֹשֻׁעַ
אֶל־כָּל־הָעָם, כֹּה אָמַר ה' אֱלֹהֵי יִשְׂרָאֵל: בְּעֵבֶר
הַנָּהָר יָשְׁבוּ אֲבוֹתֵיכֶם מֵעוֹלָם, תֶּרַח אֲבִי אַבְרָהָם
וַאֲבִי נָחוֹר, וַיַּעַבְדוּ אֱלֹהִים אֲחֵרִים.

וָאֶקַּח אֶת־אֲבִיכֶם אֶת־אַבְרָהָם מֵעֵבֶר הַנָּהָר וָאוֹלֵךְ
אוֹתוֹ בְּכָל־אֶרֶץ כְּנָעַן, וָאַרְבֶּה אֶת־זַרְעוֹ וָאֶתֶּן לוֹ
אֶת־יִצְחָק, וָאֶתֵּן לְיִצְחָק אֶת־יַעֲקֹב וְאֶת־עֵשָׂו. וָאֶתֵּן
לְעֵשָׂו אֶת־הַר שֵׂעִיר לָרֶשֶׁת אֹתוֹ, וְיַעֲקֹב וּבָנָיו
יָרְדוּ מִצְרָיִם.

[x] *Joshua* 24:2-4.

In the Beginning Our Fathers Wast Idol Worshipers

From the beginning, our ancestors wast idol worshipers. And now, the lodging hath brought us close to His worship, as tis stated, Yehoshua hath said to the whole people, so hath said the Lord, God of Israel, "Over the river didst thy ancestors dwell from at each moment, Terach the father of Avraham and the father of Nachor, and they worshiped dirty gods.[95]

And I tooketh thy father, Avraham, from over the river and I madeth him walketh in all the land of Canaan and I increased his seed and I gaveth him Yitschak. And I gaveth to Yitschak, Ya'akov, and Esav. And I gaveth to Esav, Mount Seir in order that he] inherit such a haven[96]; and Yaakov and his sons wenteth down to Egypt."

95   *Cymbeline*, Act 3, Scene 7.

96   *Ibid*, Act 3, Scene 2.

בָּרוּךְ שׁוֹמֵר הַבְטָחָתוֹ לְיִשְׂרָאֵל, בָּרוּךְ הוּא.
שֶׁהַקָּדוֹשׁ בָּרוּךְ הוּא חִשַּׁב אֶת־הַקֵּץ, לַעֲשׂוֹת כְּמוֹ
שֶׁאָמַר לְאַבְרָהָם אָבִינוּ בִּבְרִית בֵּין הַבְּתָרִים,
שֶׁנֶּאֱמַר: [xi] וַיֹּאמֶר לְאַבְרָם, יָדֹעַ תֵּדַע כִּי־גֵר יִהְיֶה
זַרְעֲךָ בְּאֶרֶץ לֹא לָהֶם, וַעֲבָדוּם וְעִנּוּ אֹתָם אַרְבַּע
מֵאוֹת שָׁנָה. וְגַם אֶת־הַגּוֹי אֲשֶׁר יַעֲבֹדוּ דָּן אָנֹכִי
וְאַחֲרֵי־כֵן יֵצְאוּ בִּרְכֻשׁ גָּדוֹל.

מכסה המצה ומגביה את הכוס בידו, ואומר:

וְהִיא שֶׁעָמְדָה לַאֲבוֹתֵינוּ וְלָנוּ. שֶׁלֹּא אֶחָד בִּלְבָד
עָמַד עָלֵינוּ לְכַלּוֹתֵנוּ, אֶלָּא שֶׁבְּכָל דּוֹר וָדוֹר
עוֹמְדִים עָלֵינוּ לְכַלּוֹתֵנוּ, וְהַקָּדוֹשׁ בָּרוּךְ הוּא
מַצִּילֵנוּ מִיָּדָם.

xi *Genesis* 15:13-14.

Blessed beest the One who layeth no blame upon His promise[97] to Israel, blessed beest He since the Holy One, blessed beest He, calculated the end of the exile, to doeth as He hath said to Avraham, our father, in the Covenant between the Pieces, as tis stated, And He hath said to Avram, 'thou should surely knoweth that thy seed wilt beest a stranger in a land that is not theirs, and they wilt enslave them and afflict them four hundred years. And eke that nation for which they shalt toil shall I play judge, and executioner,[98] and afterwards they wilt wend out with much property.'"

He covereth the unleavened breads and lifteth up the cup and sayeth:

And tis this that hath stoodeth for our ancestors and for us, since tis not only one person or nation that hath stoodeth against us to destroy us, but rather in each generation, they standeth against us to destroy us, but the Holy One, blessed beest He, rescues us from their hand.

---

97   *Macbeth*, Act 3, Scene 4.
98   *Cymbeline*, Act 4, Scene 2.

הַצְהָרַת הַפֵּרוֹת הָרִאשׁוֹנָה

יניח הכוס מידו ויגלה אֶת המצות.

צֵא וּלְמַד מַה בִּקֵּשׁ לָבָן הָאֲרַמִּי לַעֲשׂוֹת לְיַעֲקֹב אָבִינוּ: שֶׁפַּרְעֹה לֹא גָזַר אֶלָּא עַל הַזְּכָרִים, וְלָבָן בִּקֵּשׁ לַעֲקֹר אֶת־הַכֹּל. שֶׁנֶּאֱמַר:[xii] אֲרַמִּי אֹבֵד אָבִי, וַיֵּרֶד מִצְרַיְמָה וַיָּגָר שָׁם בִּמְתֵי מְעָט, וַיְהִי שָׁם לְגוֹי גָּדוֹל, עָצוּם וָרָב.

וַיֵּרֶד מִצְרַיְמָה – אָנוּס עַל פִּי הַדִּבּוּר. וַיָּגָר שָׁם. מְלַמֵּד שֶׁלֹּא יָרַד יַעֲקֹב אָבִינוּ לְהִשְׁתַּקֵּעַ בְּמִצְרַיִם אֶלָּא לָגוּר שָׁם, שֶׁנֶּאֱמַר:[xiii] וַיֹּאמְרוּ אֶל־פַּרְעֹה, לָגוּר בָּאָרֶץ בָּאנוּ, כִּי אֵין מִרְעֶה לַצֹּאן אֲשֶׁר לַעֲבָדֶיךָ, כִּי כָבֵד הָרָעָב בְּאֶרֶץ כְּנָעַן. וְעַתָּה יֵשְׁבוּ־נָא עֲבָדֶיךָ בְּאֶרֶץ גֹּשֶׁן.

[xii] Deuteronomy 26:5.
[xiii] Genesis 47:4.

Fruits that Blossom First[99]
Declaration

He putteth down the cup from his hand and uncovereth the unleavened bread.

Wend out and learneth now, for all,[100] what Lavan the Aramean sought to doeth to Ya'akov, our father, since Pharaoh only decreed on the males but Lavan sought to uproot the whole. As tis stated, "An Aramean wast destroying mine father and he wenteth down to Egypt, and he resided thither with a small number and he becameth thither a nation, most wondrous, powerful and numerous."

"And he wenteth down to Egypt" helpless on account of the word in which God toldeth Avraham that his descendants would hast to wend into exile. "And he resided there." This teachest that Ya'akov, our father, didst not wend down to settle in Egypt, but rather only to reside thither, as tis stated, "And they hath said to Pharaoh, To reside in the land hast we cometh, since thither is not enough pasture for thy servant's flocks, since the famine is heavy in the land of Canaan, and now please grant that your servants should dwell in the Land of Goshen."

---

99 *Othello*, Act 2, Scene 3.
100 *Cymbeline*, Act 2, Scene 3.

בְּמְתֵי מְעָט. כְּמָה שֶׁנֶּאֱמַר: [xiv] בְּשִׁבְעִים נֶפֶשׁ יָרְדוּ אֲבוֹתֶיךָ מִצְרָיְמָה, וְעַתָּה שָׂמְךָ ה' אֱלֹהֶיךָ כְּכוֹכְבֵי הַשָּׁמַיִם לָרֹב.

וַיְהִי שָׁם לְגוֹי. מְלַמֵּד שֶׁהָיוּ יִשְׂרָאֵל מְצֻיָּנִים שָׁם. גָּדוֹל עָצוּם – כְּמָה שֶׁנֶּאֱמַר: [xv] וּבְנֵי יִשְׂרָאֵל פָּרוּ וַיִּשְׁרְצוּ וַיִּרְבּוּ וַיַּעַצְמוּ בִּמְאֹד מְאֹד, וַתִּמָּלֵא הָאָרֶץ אֹתָם.

וָרָב. כְּמָה שֶׁנֶּאֱמַר: [xvi] רְבָבָה כְּצֶמַח הַשָּׂדֶה נְתַתִּיךְ, וַתִּרְבִּי וַתִּגְדְּלִי וַתָּבֹאִי בַּעֲדִי עֲדָיִים, שָׁדַיִם נָכֹנוּ וּשְׂעָרֵךְ צִמֵּחַ, וְאַתְּ עֵרֹם וְעֶרְיָה. וָאֶעֱבֹר עָלַיִךְ וָאֶרְאֵךְ מִתְבּוֹסֶסֶת בְּדָמָיִךְ, וָאֹמַר לָךְ בְּדָמַיִךְ חֲיִי, וָאֹמַר לָךְ בְּדָמַיִךְ חֲיִי.

וַיָּרֵעוּ אֹתָנוּ הַמִּצְרִים וַיְעַנּוּנוּ, [xvii] וַיִּתְּנוּ עָלֵינוּ עֲבֹדָה קָשָׁה. וַיָּרֵעוּ אֹתָנוּ הַמִּצְרִים – כְּמָה שֶׁנֶּאֱמַר: [xviii] הָבָה נִתְחַכְּמָה לוֹ פֶּן יִרְבֶּה, וְהָיָה כִּי תִקְרֶאנָה מִלְחָמָה וְנוֹסַף גַּם הוּא עַל שֹׂנְאֵינוּ וְנִלְחַם־בָּנוּ, וְעָלָה מִן־הָאָרֶץ.

xiv Deuteronomy 10:22.
xv Exodus 1:7.
xvi *Ezekiel* 16:7.
xvii Deuteronomy 26:6.
xviii *Ezekiel* 1:10.

"As a small number" as tis stated, "With seventy souls didst thy ancestors cometh down to Egypt, and now the Lord thy God hath madeth thee as numerous as all the number of the stars give light."[101]

"And he becameth thither a nation" this teachest that Israel became distinguishable thither. "Great, powerful" as tis stated, "And the Children of Israel multiplied and swarmed and hath grown numerous and stout, most exceedingly and the land becameth full of them."

"And numerous" as tis stated, "I hast given thee to beest numerous as the vegetation of the field, and thee increased and hath grown so catching and becameth highly ornamented, thy breasts wast setteth and thy hair hath grown so catching,[102] but thee wast a naked subject to the weeping clouds,[103] and barren, barren, barren."[104]

"And the Egyptians didst lack valor to us" as tis stated "Let us beest wise towards him, lest he multiply and twill beest that at which hour war is called, he too wilt join with our enemies and square against us and wend up from the land."

101 *Antony and Cleopatra*, Act 3, Scene 2.
102 *Henry VIII*, Act 1, Scene 3.
103 *Henry IV*, Part II, Act 1, Scene 3.
104 *Ibid*, Act 5, Scene 3.

וַיְעַנּוּנוּ. כְּמָה שֶׁנֶּאֱמַר:[xix] וַיָּשִׂימוּ עָלָיו שָׂרֵי מִסִּים
לְמַעַן עַנֹּתוֹ בְּסִבְלֹתָם. וַיִּבֶן עָרֵי מִסְכְּנוֹת לְפַרְעֹה.
אֶת־פִּתֹם וְאֶת־רַעַמְסֵס.

וַיִּתְּנוּ עָלֵינוּ עֲבֹדָה קָשָׁה. כְּמָה שֶׁנֶּאֱמַר:[xx] וַיַּעֲבִדוּ
מִצְרַיִם אֶת־בְּנֵי יִשְׂרָאֵל בְּפָרֶךְ.

וַנִּצְעַק אֶל־ה' אֱלֹהֵי אֲבֹתֵינוּ, וַיִּשְׁמַע ה' אֶת־קֹלֵנוּ,
וַיַּרְא אֶת־עָנְיֵנוּ וְאֶת־עֲמָלֵנוּ וְאֶת לַחֲצֵנוּ[xxi].

וַנִּצְעַק אֶל־ה' אֱלֹהֵי אֲבֹתֵינוּ – כְּמָה שֶׁנֶּאֱמַר:[xxii]
וַיְהִי בַיָּמִים הָרַבִּים הָהֵם וַיָּמָת מֶלֶךְ מִצְרַיִם,
וַיֵּאָנְחוּ בְנֵי־יִשְׂרָאֵל מִ־הָעֲבוֹדָה וַיִּזְעָקוּ, וַתַּעַל
שַׁוְעָתָם אֶל־הָאֱלֹהִים מִן הָעֲבֹדָה.

וַיִּשְׁמַע ה' אֶת קֹלֵנוּ. כְּמָה שֶׁנֶּאֱמַר:[xxiii] וַיִּשְׁמַע
אֱלֹהִים אֶת־נַאֲקָתָם, וַיִּזְכֹּר אֱלֹהִים אֶת־בְּרִיתוֹ אֶת־
אַבְרָהָם, אֶת־יִצְחָק וְאֶת־יַעֲקֹב.

xix Exodus 1:11.
xx Ibid.
xxi Deuteronomy 26:7.
xxii Exodus 2:23.
xxiii Exodus 2:24.

"And afflicted us" as is stated, "And they placed upon him leaders o'er the work-tax in order to afflict them with their burdens; and they hath built storage cities, Pithom and Ra'amses."

"And putteth upon us hard work" as tis stated, "And they enslaved the children of Israel with breaking work."

"And we cried, wherefore art thou[105] out to the Lord, the God of our ancestors, and the Lord hath heard the sound and fury[106] of our voice, and He saw our affliction, and our double, double, toil and trouble,[107] and our duress."

"And we cried out to the Lord, the God of our ancestors" as tis stated; "And twas in those most wondrous days that the king of Egypt hath ran mad and died[108] and the Children of Israel sighed from the work and yelled out,[109] and their supplication wenteth up to God from the work."

"And the Lord hath heard our voice" as tis stated "And God hath heard their deadly groan, like life and death's departing,[110] and God recalled His covenant with Avraham and with Yitschak and with Ya'akov."

---

105   *Romeo and Juliet*, Act 2, Scene 2.

106   *Macbeth*, Act 5, Scene 5.

107   *Ibid*, Act 4, Scene 1.

108   *Henry VIII*, Act 2, Scene 2.

109   *Macbeth*, Act 4, Scene 3.

110   *Henry VI*, Part III, Act 2, Scene 6.

וַיַּרְא אֶת־עָנְיֵנוּ. זוֹ פְּרִישׁוּת דֶּרֶךְ אֶרֶץ, כְּמָה שֶׁנֶּאֱמַר:[xxiv] וַיַּרְא אֱלֹהִים אֶת בְּנֵי־יִשְׂרָאֵל וַיֵּדַע אֱלֹהִים.

וְאֶת־עֲמָלֵנוּ. אֵלּוּ הַבָּנִים. כְּמָה שֶׁנֶּאֱמַר:[xxv] כָּל־הַבֵּן הַיִּלּוֹד הַיְאֹרָה תַּשְׁלִיכֻהוּ וְכָל־הַבַּת תְּחַיּוּן.

וְאֶת לַחֲצֵנוּ. זֶה הַדְּחַק, כְּמָה שֶׁנֶּאֱמַר:[xxvi] וְגַם־רָאִיתִי אֶת־הַלַּחַץ אֲשֶׁר מִצְרַיִם לֹחֲצִים אֹתָם.

וַיּוֹצִאֵנוּ ה' מִמִּצְרַיִם בְּיָד חֲזָקָה, וּבִזְרֹעַ נְטוּיָה, וּבְמֹרָא גָּדֹל, וּבְאֹתוֹת וּבְמֹפְתִים[xxvii].

xxiv *Exodus* 2:25.
xxv *Exodus* 1:24.
xxvi *Exodus* 3:9.
xxvii Deuteronomy 26:8.

"And He saw our affliction" this [refers to] the separation from the way of the world, as tis stated, "And God saw the Children of Israel and God kneweth."

"And forspent with toil"[111] this [refers to the killing of the] sons, as tis stated; "Every knave that is born, throweth him into the Nile and every wench thee shalt keepeth alive."

"And our duress"—this [refers to] the pressure, as tis stated, "And I eke saw the duress that the Egyptians art applying on them."

"And the Lord of all tooketh us out of Egypt with a stout and proud[112] hand and with his forearms outstretched[113] and with most wondrous awe and with comfortable good-presaging signs,[114] ay, and greater wonders than that."[115]

III   *Henry VI*, Part III, Act 2, Scene 3.
112   *Henry VI*, Part II, Act 1, Scene 1.
113   *Troilus and Cressida*, Act 3, Scene 3.
114   *King Edward III*, Act 3, Scene 3.
115   *As You Like It*, Act 5, Scene 2.

וַיּוֹצִאֵנוּ ה' מִמִּצְרַיִם. לֹא עַל־יְדֵי מַלְאָךְ, וְלֹא עַל־יְדֵי שָׂרָף, וְלֹא עַל־יְדֵי שָׁלִיחַ, אֶלָּא הַקָּדוֹשׁ בָּרוּךְ הוּא בִּכְבוֹדוֹ וּבְעַצְמוֹ. שֶׁנֶּאֱמַר: [xxviii] וְעָבַרְתִּי בְאֶרֶץ מִצְרַיִם בַּלַּיְלָה הַזֶּה, וְהִכֵּיתִי כָל־בְּכוֹר בְּאֶרֶץ מִצְרַיִם מֵאָדָם וְעַד בְּהֵמָה, וּבְכָל אֱלֹהֵי מִצְרַיִם אֶעֱשֶׂה שְׁפָטִים. אֲנִי ה.'

וְעָבַרְתִּי בְאֶרֶץ מִצְרַיִם בַּלַּיְלָה הַזֶּה – אֲנִי וְלֹא מַלְאָךְ; וְהִכֵּיתִי כָל בְּכוֹר בְּאֶרֶץ־מִצְרַיִם. אֲנִי וְלֹא שָׂרָף; וּבְכָל־אֱלֹהֵי מִצְרַיִם אֶעֱשֶׂה שְׁפָטִים. אֲנִי וְלֹא הַשָּׁלִיחַ; אֲנִי ה.' אֲנִי הוּא וְלֹא אַחֵר.

xxviii *Exodus* 12:12.

"And the Lord tooketh us out of Egypt." not through, by Jupiter, an angel[116] and not through a seraph and not through a messenger from the galleys,[117] but [directly by] the Holy One, blessed beest He, Himself, as tis stated, "And I wilt passeth through the Land of Egypt on that night and I wilt against all the firstborn in the Land of Egypt,[118] from men to those pampered animals[119]; and with all the gods of Egypt, I wilt maketh judgments, I am the Lord."

"And I wilt passeth through the Land of Egypt" I and not an angel of the air.[120] "And I wilt smite every firstborn" I and not a seraph. "And with all the gods of Egypt, I wilt maketh judgments." I and not a messenger. "I am the Lord." For I am He[121] and thither is no other.[122]

116   *Cymbeline*, Act 3, Scene 7.
117   *Othello*, Act 1, Scene 3.
118   *As You Like It*, Act 2, Scene 5.
119   *Much Ado About Nothing*, Act 4, Scene 1.
120   *The Two Noble Kinsmen*, Act 1, Scene 1.
121   *As You Like It*, Act 5, Scene 1.
122   *Othello*, Act 3, Scene 4.

בְּיָד חֲזָקָה. זוֹ הַדֶּבֶר, כְּמָה שֶׁנֶּאֱמַר:[xxix] הִנֵּה יַד־ה' הוֹיָה בְּמִקְנְךָ אֲשֶׁר בַּשָּׂדֶה, בַּסּוּסִים, בַּחֲמֹרִים, בַּגְּמַלִּים, בַּבָּקָר וּבַצֹּאן, דֶּבֶר כָּבֵד מְאֹד.

וּבִזְרֹעַ נְטוּיָה. זוֹ הַחֶרֶב, כְּמָה שֶׁנֶּאֱמַר:[xxx] וְחַרְבּוֹ שְׁלוּפָה בְּיָדוֹ, נְטוּיָה עַל־יְרוּשָׁלָיִם.

וּבְמוֹרָא גָדֹל. זוֹ גִּלּוּי שְׁכִינָה. כְּמָה שֶׁנֶּאֱמַר,[xxxi] אוֹ הֲנִסָּה אֱלֹהִים לָבוֹא לָקַחַת לוֹ גוֹי מִקֶּרֶב גּוֹי בְּמַסֹּת בְּאֹתֹת וּבְמוֹפְתִים וּבְמִלְחָמָה וּבְיָד חֲזָקָה וּבִזְרֹעַ נְטוּיָה וּבְמוֹרָאִים גְּדֹלִים כְּכֹל אֲשֶׁר־עָשָׂה לָכֶם ה' אֱלֹהֵיכֶם בְּמִצְרַיִם לְעֵינֶיךָ.

xxix *Exodus* 9:3.
xxx 1 Chronicles 21:16.
xxxi Deuteronomy 4:34.

"With a stout hand." This [refers to] the pestilence, as tis stated, "Behold the hand of the Lord is upon thy herds that art in the field, upon the horses, upon the donkeys, upon the camels, upon the cattle, and upon the flocks, [there wilt be] a very heavy pestilence, the most infectious pestilence upon thee."[123]

"And with an outstretched forearm." this [refers to] the sword, as tis stated, "And his sword wast drawn in his hand, leaning over Jerusalem."

"And with most wondrous awe" this [refers to the revelation of] the Divine Presence, as tis stated, "Or didst God tryeth to taketh for Himself a nation from within a nation with enigmas, with signs and with wonders and with war and with a stout hand and with an outstretched forearm and with most wondrous acts, like all that the Lord, thy God, didst for thee in Egypt like a beacon fired to amaze thy eyes."[124]

123 *Antony and Cleopatra*, Act 2, Scene 5.
124 *Pericles*, Act 1, Scene 4.

וּבְאֹתוֹת. זֶה הַמַּטֶּה, כְּמָה שֶׁנֶּאֱמַר: [xxxii] וְאֶת הַמַּטֶּה הַזֶּה תִּקַּח בְּיָדֶךָ, אֲשֶׁר תַּעֲשֶׂה־בּוֹ אֶת הָאֹתוֹת.

וּבְמֹפְתִים. זֶה הַדָּם, כְּמָה שֶׁנֶּאֱמַר: [xxxiii] וְנָתַתִּי מוֹפְתִים בַּשָּׁמַיִם וּבָאָרֶץ.

[xxxii] *Exodus* 4:17.

"And with signs" this [refers to] the staff he threw,[125] as tis stated, "And this staff thee shalt taketh in thy hand, that with it thee wilt perform signs."

"And with wonders" this [refers to] the blood, as tis stated, "And I wilt lodge mine wonders in the skies and in the earth."

125   *Henry IV*, Part II, Act 4, Scene I.

עֶשֶׂר מַכּוֹת

[חלק מהנה! הבעל מקבל שוב את תשומת הלב של כולם, וכל הנוכחים משתתפים.]

כשאומר דם ואש ותימרות עשן, עשר המכות ודצ"ך עד"ש באח"ב – ישפוך מן הכוס מעט יין.

דָּם וָאֵשׁ וְתִימְרוֹת עָשָׁן.

[מיץ ענבים נמצא כעת בכל מקום. האישה נסערת.]

דָּבָר אַחֵר: בְּיָד חֲזָקָה שְׁתַּיִם, וּבִזְרֹעַ נְטוּיָה שְׁתַּיִם, וּבְמֹרָא גָּדֹל – שְׁתַּיִם, וּבְאֹתוֹת – שְׁתַּיִם, וּבְמֹפְתִים – שְׁתַּיִם.

אֵלּוּ עֶשֶׂר מַכּוֹת שֶׁהֵבִיא הַקָּדוֹשׁ בָּרוּךְ הוּא עַל־הַמִּצְרִים בְּמִצְרַיִם, וְאֵלּוּ הֵן:

[האישה מתכוננת לבלאגן שעומד לקרות.]

The Ten Plagues

[Fun part! The husband has everyone's attention again, and all present participate.]

And whence he sayeth, "blood and sword and fire[126] *and pillars of smoke and bounce"*[127] *and the ten plagues and "detsakh," "adash," and "ba'achab," he should pour out a little wine from his cup.*

Blood and fire and pillars of smoke.

[Grape juice is now everywhere. The wife cringes.]

Another. "With a stout hand" two. "And with an outstretched forearm" two. "And with most wondrous awe" two. "And with signs" two. "And with wonders" two.

These art [the] ten plagues that the Holy One, blessed beest the great He,[128] hath brought on the Egyptians in Egypt and those art.

[The wife braces for the mess that's about to happen.]

---

126 *Henry V*, Act 1, Scene 2.
127 *King John*, Act 2, Scene 1.
128 *The Winter's Tale*, Act 3, Scene 2.

דָּם

צְפַרְדֵּעַ

כִּנִּים

עָרוֹב

דֶּבֶר

שְׁחִין

בָּרָד

אַרְבֶּה

חֹשֶׁךְ

מַכַּת בְּכוֹרוֹת

רַבִּי יְהוּדָה הָיָה נוֹתֵן בָּהֶם סִמָּנִים:
דְּצַ"ךְ עַדַ"שׁ בְּאַחַ"ב.

The Hazard of Much Blood[129]

The Swimming Frog, The Toad[130]

The Louse of a Lazar[131]

The Evil Mixture of Disordered Animals[132]

Armies of Pestilence[133]

Boils and Bubbles[134]

All Hail[135]

Lucious Locusts[136]

Hideous Darkness[137]

Slaying of the Firstborn of Egypt[138]

Clergyman Yehuda wast accustomed to giving mnemonics: Detsakh, Adash, Beachav.

129 *Coriolanus*, Act 3, Scene 2.

130 *King Lear*, Act 3, Scene 5.

131 *Troilus and Cressida*, Act 5, Scene 1.

132 *Ibid*, Act 1, Scene 3.

133 *Richard II*, Act 3, Scene 3.

134 *Measure for Measure*, Act 5, Scene 1.

135 *Julius Caesar*, Act 2, Scene 2.

136 *Othello*, Act 1, Scene 3.

137 *Twelfth Night*, Act 4, Scene 2.

138 *As You Like It*, Act 2, Scene 5.

רַבִּי יוֹסֵי הַגְּלִילִי אוֹמֵר: מִנַּיִן אַתָּה אוֹמֵר שֶׁלָּקוּ
הַמִּצְרִים בְּמִצְרַיִם עֶשֶׂר מַכּוֹת וְעַל הַיָּם לָקוּ
חֲמִשִּׁים מַכּוֹת? בְּמִצְרַיִם מַה הוּא אוֹמֵר? וַיֹּאמְרוּ
הַחַרְטֻמִּם אֶל פַּרְעֹה: אֶצְבַּע אֱלֹהִים הוּא,[xxxiv] וְעַל
הַיָּם מָה הוּא אוֹמֵר? וַיַּרְא יִשְׂרָאֵל אֶת־הַיָּד הַגְּדֹלָה
אֲשֶׁר עָשָׂה ה' בְּמִצְרַיִם, וַיִּירְאוּ הָעָם אֶת־ה',
וַיַּאֲמִינוּ בַּיָי וּבְמֹשֶׁה עַבְדּוֹ.[xxxv] כַּמָּה לָקוּ בְאֶצְבַּע?
עֶשֶׂר מַכּוֹת. אֱמוֹר מֵעַתָּה: בְּמִצְרַיִם לָקוּ עֶשֶׂר
מַכּוֹת וְעַל הַיָּם לָקוּ חֲמִשִּׁים מַכּוֹת.

רַבִּי אֱלִיעֶזֶר אוֹמֵר: מִנַּיִן שֶׁכָּל־מַכָּה וּמַכָּה שֶׁהֵבִיא
הַקָּדוֹשׁ בָּרוּךְ הוּא עַל הַמִּצְרִים בְּמִצְרַיִם הָיְתָה שֶׁל
אַרְבַּע מַכּוֹת? שֶׁנֶּאֱמַר:[xxxvi] יְשַׁלַּח־בָּם חֲרוֹן אַפּוֹ,
עֶבְרָה וָזַעַם וְצָרָה, מִשְׁלַחַת מַלְאֲכֵי רָעִים. עֶבְרָה –
אַחַת, וָזַעַם – שְׁתַּיִם, וְצָרָה – שָׁלֹשׁ, מִשְׁלַחַת
מַלְאֲכֵי רָעִים – אַרְבַּע. אֱמוֹר מֵעַתָּה: בְּמִצְרַיִם לָקוּ
אַרְבָּעִים מַכּוֹת וְעַל הַיָּם לָקוּ מָאתַיִם מַכּוֹת.

[xxxiv] *Exodus* 8:15.
[xxxv] *Exodus* 14:31.
[xxxvi] *Psalms* 78:49.

Clergyman Yose Hagelili sayeth, "From whither can thee sayeth that the Egyptians wast struck with ten plagues in Egypt and struck with fifty plagues at empire of the sea?[139] In Egypt, what doest it state? Then the magicians hath said unto Pharaoh, "This is the digit of God." And athwart the Sea,[140] what doest it state? And Israel saw the Lord's most wondrous hand that He used upon the Egyptians, and the people feared the Lord; and they hath believed in the Lord, and in Moshe, His most obedient servant.[141] How many wast those struck with the digit? Ten plagues. Thee can sayeth from hither that in Egypt, they wast struck with ten plagues and into the bosom of the sea,[142] they wast struck with fifty plagues."

Clergyman Eliezer sayeth, "From whither that every plague that the Holy One, blessed beest He, hath brought upon the Egyptians in Egypt wast of four plagues? As tis stated, 'He hath sent upon them the fierceness of His snuffs, heap of wrath,[143] and moody discontented fury,[144] and exceeding trouble,[145] a sending of messengers of the evil that men do.'[146] 'Wrath' one. 'And fury' two. 'And trouble' three. 'A sending of messengers of evil' four. Thee can sayeth from hither that in Egypt, they wast struck with forty plagues and at the rising bubble in the sea,[147] they wast struck with two hundred plagues."

---

139 *Antony and Cleopatra*, Act 1, Scene 2.
140 *Henry V*, Act 5, Chorus.
141 *All's Well That Ends Well*, Act 2, Scene 5.
142 *Henry VI, Part II*, Act 4, Scene 1.
143 *Henry VI, Part II*, Act 5, Scene 1.
144 *Henry VI, Part I*, Act 3, Scene 1.
145 *Henry VI, Part II*, Act 5, Scene 1.
146 *Julius Caesar*, Act 3, Scene 2.
147 *Edward III*, Act 5, Scene 1.

רַבִּי עֲקִיבָא אוֹמֵר: מִנַּיִן שֶׁכָּל־מַכָּה וּמַכָּה שֶׁהֵבִיא הַקָּדוֹשׁ בָּרוּךְ הוּא עַל הַמִּצְרִים בְּמִצְרַיִם הָיְתָה שֶׁל חָמֵשׁ מַכּוֹת? שֶׁנֶּאֱמַר:[xxxvii] יְשַׁלַּח־בָּם חֲרוֹן אַפּוֹ, עֶבְרָה וָזַעַם וְצָרָה, מִשְׁלַחַת מַלְאֲכֵי רָעִים. חֲרוֹן אַפּוֹ – אַחַת, עֶבְרָה – שְׁתַּיִם, וָזַעַם – שָׁלוֹשׁ, וְצָרָה – אַרְבַּע, מִשְׁלַחַת מַלְאֲכֵי רָעִים – חָמֵשׁ. אֱמוֹר מֵעַתָּה: בְּמִצְרַיִם לָקוּ חֲמִשִּׁים מַכּוֹת וְעַל הַיָּם לָקוּ חֲמִשִּׁים וּמָאתַיִם מַכּוֹת.

───────
[xxxvii] Ibid.

Clergyman Akiva sayeth, "From whither that every plague that the Holy One, blessed beest He, hath brought upon the Egyptians in Egypt wast of five plagues? As tis stated, 'He hath sent upon them the fierceness of His snuffs, wrath, and fury, and trouble, a sending of messengers of evil.' 'The fierceness of His anger' one. 'Wrath' two. 'And fury' three. 'And trouble' four. 'A sending of messengers of evil' five. Thee can sayeth from hither that in Egypt, they wast struck with fifty plagues and at the sea, they wast struck with two hundred and fifty plagues."

דַּיֵּנוּ

כַּמָּה מַעֲלוֹת טוֹבוֹת לַמָּקוֹם עָלֵינוּ!

אִלּוּ הוֹצִיאָנוּ מִמִּצְרַיִם וְלֹא עָשָׂה בָהֶם שְׁפָטִים,
דַּיֵּנוּ.

אִלּוּ עָשָׂה בָהֶם שְׁפָטִים, וְלֹא עָשָׂה בֵאלֹהֵיהֶם,
דַּיֵּנוּ.

אִלּוּ עָשָׂה בֵאלֹהֵיהֶם, וְלֹא הָרַג אֶת־בְּכוֹרֵיהֶם,
דַּיֵּנוּ.

אִלּוּ הָרַג אֶת־בְּכוֹרֵיהֶם וְלֹא נָתַן לָנוּ אֶת־מָמוֹנָם,
דַּיֵּנוּ.

אִלּוּ נָתַן לָנוּ אֶת־מָמוֹנָם וְלֹא קָרַע לָנוּ אֶת־הַיָּם,
דַּיֵּנוּ.

אִלּוּ קָרַע לָנוּ אֶת־הַיָּם וְלֹא הֶעֱבִירָנוּ בְּתוֹכוֹ
בֶּחָרָבָה, דַּיֵּנוּ.

Enough for Us

[Everyone gets a stanza, except for those arguing about what "Enough for us" means exactly.]

How many degrees of thy valor and thy heart[148] didst the lodging bestow upon us!

If it be true[149] that He hadst taken us out of Egypt and not madeth judgements on them, it would hast been enough for us.

If it be true[150] that He hadst madeth judgments on them and hadst not madeth them on their gods, it would hast been enough for us.

If He hadst madeth them on their gods and hadst not killed their firstborn, it would hast been enough for us.

If He hadst killed their firstborn and hadst not given us their wage, it would hast been enough for us.

If it be true[151] that He hadst given us their wage and hadst not split the sea for us, it would hast been enough for us.

If He hadst split the sea for us and hadst not taken us through it on dry land, it would hast been enough for us.

---

148 *King Lear*, Act 5, Scene 3.
149 *As You Like It*, Act 4, Scene 5.
150 *Cymbeline*, Act 1, Scene 7.
151 *King Lear*, Act 2, Scene 1.

אִלּוּ הֶעֱבִירָנוּ בְּתוֹכוֹ בֶּחָרָבָה וְלֹא שִׁקַּע צָרֵנוּ בְּתוֹכוֹ דַּיֵּנוּ.

אִלּוּ שִׁקַּע צָרֵנוּ בְּתוֹכוֹ וְלֹא סִפֵּק צָרְכֵּנוּ בַּמִּדְבָּר אַרְבָּעִים שָׁנָה דַּיֵּנוּ.

אִלּוּ סִפֵּק צָרְכֵּנוּ בְּמִדְבָּר אַרְבָּעִים שָׁנָה וְלֹא הֶאֱכִילָנוּ אֶת־הַמָּן דַּיֵּנוּ.

אִלּוּ הֶאֱכִילָנוּ אֶת־הַמָּן וְלֹא נָתַן לָנוּ אֶת־הַשַּׁבָּת, דַּיֵּנוּ.

אִלּוּ נָתַן לָנוּ אֶת־הַשַּׁבָּת, וְלֹא קֵרְבָנוּ לִפְנֵי הַר סִינַי, דַּיֵּנוּ.

אִלּוּ קֵרְבָנוּ לִפְנֵי הַר סִינַי, וְלֹא נַתַן לָנוּ אֶת־הַתּוֹרָה. דַּיֵּנוּ.

אִלּוּ נָתַן לָנוּ אֶת־הַתּוֹרָה וְלֹא הִכְנִיסָנוּ לְאֶרֶץ יִשְׂרָאֵל, דַּיֵּנוּ.

אִלּוּ הִכְנִיסָנוּ לְאֶרֶץ יִשְׂרָאֵל וְלֹא בָנָה לָנוּ אֶת־בֵּית הַבְּחִירָה דַּיֵּנוּ.

If He hadst taken us through it on dry land and hadst not pushed down the numbers of our enemies[152] in the sea, it would hast been enough for us.

If it be true[153] that He hadst pushed down our enemies in the sea and hadst not supplied our needs in the warped slip of wilderness[154] for forty years, it would hast been enough for us.

If He hadst supplied our needs in the wilderness for forty years and hadst not fed us the manna in the way,[155] it would hast been enough for us.

If He hadst fed us the manna and hadst not given us the Sabbath, it would hast been enough for us.

If He hadst given us the Sabbath and hadst not brought us close to Mount Sinai, it would hast been enough for us.

If it be true that He hadst brought us close to Mount Sinai and hadst not given us the Torah, it would hast been enough for us.

If He hadst given us the Torah and hadst not brought us into the land of Israel, it would hast been enough for us.

If He hadst brought us into the land of Israel and hadst not built us the Chosen House, it would hast been enough for us.

---

152   *Henry IV*, Part II, Act 4, Scene 1.
153   *Pericles*, Act 1, Scene 1.
154   *Measure for Measure*, Act 3, Scene 1.
155   *The Merchant of Venice*, Act 5, Scene 1.

עַל אַחַת, כַּמָּה וְכַמָּה, טוֹבָה כְפוּלָה וּמְכֻפֶּלֶת
לַמָּקוֹם עָלֵינוּ: שֶׁהוֹצִיאָנוּ מִמִּצְרַיִם, וְעָשָׂה בָהֶם
שְׁפָטִים, וְעָשָׂה בֵאלֹהֵיהֶם, וְהָרַג אֶת־בְּכוֹרֵיהֶם,
וְנָתַן לָנוּ אֶת־מָמוֹנָם, וְקָרַע לָנוּ אֶת־הַיָּם,
וְהֶעֱבִירָנוּ בְתוֹכוֹ בֶּחָרָבָה, וְשִׁקַּע צָרֵנוּ בְּתוֹכוֹ,
וְסִפֵּק צָרְכֵּנוּ בַּמִּדְבָּר אַרְבָּעִים שָׁנָה, וְהֶאֱכִילָנוּ אֶת־
הַמָּן, וְנָתַן לָנוּ אֶת־הַשַּׁבָּת, וְקֵרְבָנוּ לִפְנֵי הַר סִינַי,
וְנַתַן לָנוּ אֶת־הַתּוֹרָה, וְהִכְנִיסָנוּ לְאֶרֶץ יִשְׂרָאֵל,
וּבָנָה לָנוּ אֶת־בֵּית הַבְּחִירָה לְכַפֵּר עַל־כָּל־
עֲוֹנוֹתֵינוּ.

How much more so is the valor that is doubled and this gift twice doubled[156] that the lodging bestowed upon us, since He tooketh us out of Egypt, and madeth judgments with them, and madeth them with their gods, and hath killed their firstborn, and gaveth us their wage, and split the sea for us, and hath brought us through it on dry land, and pushed down our enemies, and supplied our needs in the wilderness for forty years, and fed us the manna, and gaveth us the Shabbat, and brought us close to Mount Sinai, and gave us the Torah, and brought us into the brave new world[157] of Israel and built us the 'Chosen House' to atone upon all of our sins.

---

156 *King Edward III*, Act 4, Scene 7.

157 *The Tempest*, Act 5, Scene 1.

שְׁלֹשֶׁת הַדְּבָרִים שֶׁל רַבָּן גַּמְלִיאֵל

רַבָּן גַּמְלִיאֵל הָיָה אוֹמֵר: כָּל שֶׁלֹּא אָמַר שְׁלֹשָׁה דְבָרִים אֵלּוּ בַּפֶּסַח, לֹא יָצָא יְדֵי חוֹבָתוֹ, וְאֵלּוּ הֵן: פֶּסַח, מַצָּה, וּמָרוֹר.

פֶּסַח שֶׁהָיוּ אֲבוֹתֵינוּ אוֹכְלִים בִּזְמַן שֶׁבֵּית הַמִּקְדָּשׁ הָיָה קַיָּם, עַל שׁוּם מָה? עַל שׁוּם שֶׁפָּסַח הַקָּדוֹשׁ בָּרוּךְ הוּא עַל בָּתֵּי אֲבוֹתֵינוּ בְּמִצְרַיִם, שֶׁנֶּאֱמַר:xxxviii וַאֲמַרְתֶּם זֶבַח פֶּסַח הוּא לַיָי, אֲשֶׁר פָּסַח עַל בָּתֵּי בְנֵי יִשְׂרָאֵל בְּמִצְרַיִם בְּנָגְפּוֹ אֶת־מִצְרַיִם, וְאֶת־בָּתֵּינוּ הִצִּיל וַיִּקֹד הָעָם וַיִּשְׁתַּחֲווּ.

אוחז המצה בידו ומראה אותה למסובין.

---

xxxviii *Exodus* 12:27.

Clergyman of Holy Reverence[158] Gamliel's Three Things

[The husband loses everyone again, while conversation veers towards politics. Uh oh.]

Clergyman of Holy Reverence Gamliel wast accustomed to say, "Anyone who hath not said these three things on Passover hath not fulfilled his obligation, and these art those: the Passover sacrifice, unleavened bread, and bitter herb."

The Passover sacrifice that our ancestors wast accustomed to eating at which hour the Temple much surpassing[159] existed, for the sake of what? For the sake that the Holy One, blessed beest He hath passed over the homes of our ancestors in Egypt, as tis stated, "And thee shalt sayeth, 'It is the Passover sacrifice to the Lord, for He hath passed over the homes of the Children of Israel in Egypt, at which hour He smote the Egyptians, and our homes He saved.' And the people with gentle breath, but soft[160] look, knees humbly bowed[161] the head and bowed."

He holds the unleavened bread in his hand and showeth it to the others thither.

158   *Richard II*, Act 3, Scene 3.
159   *The Winter's Tale*, Act 3, Scene 1.
160   *Romeo and Juliet*, Act 2, Scene 2.
161   *Ibid*, Act 3, Scene 1.

מַצָּה זוֹ שֶׁאָנוּ אוֹכְלִים, עַל שׁוּם מַה? עַל שׁוּם שֶׁלֹּא הִסְפִּיק בְּצֵקָם שֶׁל אֲבוֹתֵינוּ לְהַחֲמִיץ עַד שֶׁנִּגְלָה עֲלֵיהֶם מֶלֶךְ מַלְכֵי הַמְּלָכִים, הַקָּדוֹשׁ בָּרוּךְ הוּא, וּגְאָלָם, שֶׁנֶּאֱמַר:xxxix וַיֹּאפוּ אֶת־הַבָּצֵק אֲשֶׁר הוֹצִיאוּ מִמִּצְרַיִם עֻגֹת מַצּוֹת, כִּי לֹא חָמֵץ, כִּי גֹרְשׁוּ מִמִּצְרַיִם וְלֹא יָכְלוּ לְהִתְמַהְמֵהַּ, וְגַם צֵדָה לֹא עָשׂוּ לָהֶם.

אוחז המרור בידו ומראה אותו למסובין.

מָרוֹר זֶה שֶׁאָנוּ אוֹכְלִים, עַל שׁוּם מַה? עַל שׁוּם שֶׁמֵּרְרוּ הַמִּצְרִים אֶת־חַיֵּי אֲבוֹתֵינוּ בְּמִצְרַיִם, שֶׁנֶּאֱמַר:xl וַיְמָרְרוּ אֶת חַיֵּיהֶם בַּעֲבֹדָה קָשָׁה, בְּחֹמֶר וּבִלְבֵנִים וּבְכָל־עֲבֹדָה בַּשָּׂדֶה אֵת כָּל עֲבֹדָתָם אֲשֶׁר עָבְדוּ בָהֶם בְּפָרֶךְ.

xxxix Exodus 12:39.
xl Ibid 1:14.

This unleavened bread that we art eating, for the sake of what? For the sake that our ancestors' dough wast not yet able to rise, ere the supreme King of the kings of kings,[162] the Holy One, blessed beest He, revealed Himself to them and redeemed them, as tis stated," And they baked the dough which they hath brought out of Egypt into unleavened bread cakes, since it didst not rise, because they wast expelled from Egypt, and could not tarry, neither hadst they madeth for themselves provisions."

He holds the bitter herb in his hand and showeth it to the others thither.

This bitter greens that we art eating, for the sake of what? For the sake [to commemorate] that the Egyptians embittered the lives of our ancestors in Egypt, as tis stated, "And they madeth their lives bitter with hard service, in mortar and in brick, and in all manner of service in the field; in all their service, wherein they madeth them serveth with rigor."

---

162 *Richard III*, Act 2, Scene 1.

בְּכָל־דּוֹר וָדוֹר חַיָּב אָדָם לִרְאוֹת אֶת־עַצְמוֹ כְּאִלּוּ הוּא יָצָא מִמִּצְרַיִם, שֶׁנֶּאֱמַר:[xli] וְהִגַּדְתָּ לְבִנְךָ בַּיּוֹם הַהוּא לֵאמֹר, בַּעֲבוּר זֶה עָשָׂה ה' לִי בְּצֵאתִי מִמִּצְרָיִם. לֹא אֶת־אֲבוֹתֵינוּ בִּלְבָד גָּאַל הַקָּדוֹשׁ בָּרוּךְ הוּא, אֶלָּא אַף אוֹתָנוּ גָּאַל עִמָּהֶם, שֶׁנֶּאֱמַר:[xlii] וְאוֹתָנוּ הוֹצִיא מִשָּׁם, לְמַעַן הָבִיא אוֹתָנוּ, לָתֶת לָנוּ אֶת־הָאָרֶץ אֲשֶׁר נִשְׁבַּע לַאֲבֹתֵינוּ.

[xli] *Exodus* 13:8.
[xlii] Deuteronomy 6:23.

In each and every generation, a person is obligated to see himself as if it be true that he hath left Egypt, as tis stated, "And thee shalt pray pardon me to thy son on that day: for the sake of this, didst the Lord doeth [this] for me in mine going out of Egypt." Not only our ancestors didst the Holy One, blessed beest He, redeem by some laudable attempt,[163] but rather eke us together] with them didst He redeem, as tis stated, "And He tooketh us out from thither, in order to bringeth us in, to giveth us the land which sure as death He sworeth[164] unto our fathers."

163   *Twelfth Night*, Act 3, Scene 2.
164   *Titus Andronicus*, Act I, Scene I.

מַחֲצִית הָרִאשׁוֹנָה שֶׁל הַלֵּל

לְפִיכָךְ אֲנַחְנוּ חַיָּבִים לְהוֹדוֹת, לְהַלֵּל, לְשַׁבֵּחַ,
לְפָאֵר, לְרוֹמֵם, לְהַדֵּר, לְבָרֵךְ, לְעַלֵּה וּלְקַלֵּס לְמִי
שֶׁעָשָׂה לַאֲבוֹתֵינוּ וְלָנוּ אֶת־כָּל־הַנִּסִּים הָאֵלּוּ:
הוֹצִיאָנוּ מֵעַבְדוּת לְחֵרוּת מִיָּגוֹן לְשִׂמְחָה, וּמֵאֵבֶל
לְיוֹם טוֹב, וּמֵאֲפֵלָה לְאוֹר גָּדוֹל, וּמִשִּׁעְבּוּד לִגְאֻלָּה.
וְנֹאמַר לְפָנָיו שִׁירָה חֲדָשָׁה: הַלְלוּיָהּ.

First Half of Praise

*He holdeth the cup in his hand and he covereth the unleav-
ened bread and sayeth:*

Therefore we art obligated to thank, praise, laud
be to God![165] glorify, exalt, lavish, bless, raiseth
high, and acclaim He who with love wrought these
miracles[166] for our ancestors and for us that He hath
brought us out from slavery to peace, freedom, and
liberty,[167] from a bitter touch of sorrow[168] to no such
joy on earth,[169] from mourning to [celebration of]
a festival, from darkness to most wondrous light,
and from servitude to redemption. And alloweth us
sayeth a new song ere him, Halleluyah!

165   *Henry IV, Part II*, Act 4, Scene 5.
166   *The Taming of the Shrew*, Act 5, Scene 1.
167   *Julius Caesar*, Act 3, Scene 1.
168   *All's Well That Ends Well*, Act 1, Scene 3.
169   *The Two Gentlemen of Verona*, Act 2, Scene 4.

הַלְלוּיָהּ הַלְלוּ עַבְדֵי ה', הַלְלוּ אֶת־שֵׁם ה'. יְהִי שֵׁם ה' מְבֹרָךְ מֵעַתָּה וְעַד עוֹלָם. מִמִּזְרַח שֶׁמֶשׁ עַד מְבוֹאוֹ מְהֻלָּל שֵׁם ה'. רָם עַל־כָּל־גּוֹיִם ה', עַל הַשָּׁמַיִם כְּבוֹדוֹ. מִי כַּיי אֱלֹהֵינוּ הַמַּגְבִּיהִי לָשָׁבֶת, הַמַּשְׁפִּילִי לִרְאוֹת בַּשָּׁמַיִם וּבָאָרֶץ? מְקִימִי מֵעָפָר דָּל, מֵאַשְׁפֹּת יָרִים אֶבְיוֹן, לְהוֹשִׁיבִי עִם־נְדִיבִים, עִם נְדִיבֵי עַמּוֹ. מוֹשִׁיבִי עֲקֶרֶת הַבַּיִת, אֵם הַבָּנִים שְׂמֵחָה. הַלְלוּיָהּ.[xliii]

בְּצֵאת יִשְׂרָאֵל מִמִּצְרָיִם, בֵּית יַעֲקֹב מֵעַם לֹעֵז, הָיְתָה יְהוּדָה לְקָדְשׁוֹ, יִשְׂרָאֵל מַמְשְׁלוֹתָיו. הַיָּם רָאָה וַיָּנֹס, הַיַּרְדֵּן יִסֹּב לְאָחוֹר. הֶהָרִים רָקְדוּ כְאֵילִים, גְּבָעוֹת כִּבְנֵי צֹאן. מַה לְּךָ הַיָּם כִּי תָנוּס, הַיַּרְדֵּן – תִּסֹּב לְאָחוֹר, הֶהָרִים – תִּרְקְדוּ כְאֵילִים, גְּבָעוֹת כִּבְנֵי־צֹאן. מִלְּפְנֵי אָדוֹן חוּלִי אָרֶץ, מִלְּפְנֵי אֱלוֹהַּ יַעֲקֹב. הַהֹפְכִי הַצּוּר אֲגַם־מָיִם, חַלָּמִישׁ לְמַעְיְנוֹ־מָיִם.[xliv]

[xliii] Psalms 113.
[xliv] Psalms 114.

Halleluyah! Praise, servants of the Lord, praise the name of the Lord. May the Name of the Lord beest blessed from now and still. From the rising of the sun in the East to its setting, the name of the Lord is praised. Above all nations is the Lord, His honor is above the heavens. Who is like the Lord, our God, Who sitteth on high, Who looks down upon the heavens and the earth? He bringeth up the poor out of the dirt; from the refuse heaps and piles of ruin,[170] He raiseth the destitute. To seat Him with the nobles, with the nobles of His people. He seats a barren mistress in a home, a joyous mother of children. Halleluyah!

In Israel's going out from Egypt, the house of Ya'akov from a people of foreign speech. Yehudah becameth His holy one, Israel, His whole dominion of the realm.[171] The sea saw and fled, the Jordan turned to the rear. The mountains danced like rams, the hills like young sheep. What is happening to thee, O sea, that thee art fleeing, O Jordan that thee turn to the rear, O mountains that thee dance like rams, O hills like young sheep? From ere the Master, O tremble, for you hear the lion roar,[172] O earth, from ere the Lord of Ya'akov. He who turns the boulder into a pond of water, the flint into a spring of water.

---

170   *Coriolanus*, Act 3, Scene 1.

171   *King Edward III*, Act 4, Scene 1.

172   *King John*, Act 2, Scene 1.

כּוֹס שֵׁנִי

מגביהים את הכוס עד גאל ישראל.

בָּרוּךְ אַתָּה ה' אֱלֹהֵינוּ מֶלֶךְ הָעוֹלָם, אֲשֶׁר גְּאָלָנוּ
וְגָאַל אֶת־אֲבוֹתֵינוּ מִמִּצְרַיִם, וְהִגִּיעָנוּ הַלַּיְלָה הַזֶּה
לֶאֱכָל־בּוֹ מַצָּה וּמָרוֹר. כֵּן ה' אֱלֹהֵינוּ וֵאלֹהֵי
אֲבוֹתֵינוּ יַגִּיעֵנוּ לְמוֹעֲדִים וְלִרְגָלִים אֲחֵרִים הַבָּאִים
לִקְרָאתֵנוּ לְשָׁלוֹם, שְׂמֵחִים בְּבִנְיַן עִירֶךָ וְשָׂשִׂים
בַּעֲבוֹדָתֶךָ. וְנֹאכַל שָׁם מִן הַזְּבָחִים וּמִן הַפְּסָחִים
אֲשֶׁר יַגִּיעַ דָּמָם עַל קִיר מִזְבַּחֲךָ לְרָצוֹן, וְנוֹדֶה לְךָ
שִׁיר חָדָשׁ עַל גְּאֻלָּתֵנוּ וְעַל פְּדוּת נַפְשֵׁנוּ. בָּרוּךְ
אַתָּה ה', גָּאַל יִשְׂרָאֵל.

שותים את הכוס בהסבת שמאל.

בָּרוּךְ אַתָּה ה', אֱלֹהֵינוּ מֶלֶךְ הָעוֹלָם בּוֹרֵא פְּרִי
הַגָּפֶן.

Second Cup of Wine, Sir[173]

We raiseth the cup until we reacheth "who redeemed Israel."

Blessed art thee, Lord our God, King of the universe, who redeemed us and redeemed our ancestors from Egypt, and hath brought us on this night to consume unleavened bread and bitter greens. So too, Lord our God, and God of our ancestors, bringeth us to other appointed times and holidays that wilt cometh to greet us in peace, joyful in the building of thy city and joyous in thy worship; that we shalt consume thither from the offerings and from the Passover sacrifices, the blood of which shall reach the wall of Your altar for favor, and we shall thank You with a new song upon our redemption and upon the restoration of our souls. Blessed are you, Lord, who redeemed Israel.

We sayeth the blessing below and drinketh the cup while reclining to the left.

Blessed art thee, Lord our God, who be the monarch of the fruit of the vine.[174]

---

173 *Henry IV*, Part II, Act 5, Scene 3.
174 *Antony and Cleopatra*, Act 2, Scene 7.

רָחְצָה

[כולם עוזבים את השולחן ופונים למטבח. האפיקומן נצפה במקום המוסתר החכם שלו. הבנים תופסים אותו, ומסתירים אותו, וחוזרים לתור נטילת הידיים, נראים תמימים לחלוטין. כולם חוזרים לשולחן.]

נוטלים את הידים ומברכים:

בָּרוּךְ אַתָּה ה', אֱלֹהֵינוּ מֶלֶךְ הָעוֹלָם, אֲשֶׁר קִדְּשָׁנוּ בְּמִצְוֹתָיו וְצִוָּנוּ עַל נְטִילַת יָדָיִם.

Have Need of Washing[175]

[Everyone leaves the table and heads to the kitchen. The afikoman is spotted in its clever hiding spot. The sons grab it, hide it, and return to the hand-washing queue, looking perfectly innocent. Everyone returns to the table.]

We washeth the hands and maketh the blessing:

Blessed art thee, Lord our God, King of the universe, who hath sanctified us with His commandments and hath commanded us to please Your Mightiness to wash your hands.[176]

175   *The Merry Wives of Windsor*, Act 3, Scene 3.
176   *The Taming of the Shrew*, Introduction.

מוֹצִיא מַצָּה

יקח המצות בסדר שהניחן, הפרוסה בין שתי השלמות, יאחז שלשתן בידו ויברך "המוציא" בכוונה על העליונה, ו"על אכילת מצה" בכוונה על הפרוסה. אחר כך יבצע כזית מן העליונה השלמה וכזית שני מן הפרוסה, ויטבלם במלח, ויאכל בהסבה שני הזיתים.

בָּרוּךְ אַתָּה ה', אֱלֹהֵינוּ מֶלֶךְ הָעוֹלָם הַמּוֹצִיא לֶחֶם מִן הָאָרֶץ.

בָּרוּךְ אַתָּה ה', אֱלֹהֵינוּ מֶלֶךְ הָעוֹלָם, אֲשֶׁר קִדְּשָׁנוּ בְּמִצְוֹתָיו וְצִוָּנוּ עַל אֲכִילַת מַצָּה.

Come, Bring Forth[177] Unleavened Bread

He doth take out the unleavened bread in the order that he placed them, the broken one between the two whole ones, he holds the three of them in his hand and blesses "ha-motsi" with the intention to taketh from the top one and "on eating unleavened bread" with the intention of eating from the broken one. Afterwards, he breaketh off an olive's measure from the top whole one and a second olive's measure from the broken one and he dips them into salt and consumeth both while reclining.

Blessed art thee, Lord our God, King of the universe, who bringeth forth bread from the ground like feathered Mercury.[178]

Blessed art thee, Lord our God, King of the universe, who hath sanctified us with His commandments and hath commanded us on the eating of unleavened bread.

---

177 *All's Well That Ends Well*, Act 4, Scene 3.
178 *Henry IV*, Part I, Act 4, Scene 1.

מָרוֹר

כל אחד מהמסבים לוקח כזית מרור, מטבלו בַּחֲרוֹסֶת, מנער החרוסת, מברך ואוכל בלי הסבה.

בָּרוּךְ אַתָּה ה', אֱלֹהֵינוּ מֶלֶךְ הָעוֹלָם, אֲשֶׁר קִדְּשָׁנוּ בְּמִצְוֹתָיו וְצִוָּנוּ עַל אֲכִילַת מָרוֹר.

[כולם לוקחים רק כמות זעירה של מרור אמיתי, אבל סופגים אותו בחסה וחרוסת. הבעל, בהיותו גבר גברי אלפא זכר ביג שוט לוקח רק את החומר האמיתי. הוא הופך לצבעים של מעיל החלומות המדהים של ג'וזף, אבל, למרבה המזל, מתאושש.]

Bitter Greens

All present should taketh an olive's measure of bitter greens, dippeth into the haroset, shaketh off the haroset, maketh the blessing and consumeth without reclining.

Blessed are You, Lord our God, King of the universe, who has sanctified us with His commandments and has commanded us on the eating of bitter green leaves that quiver with the cooling wind.[179]

[Everyone takes just a teeny-tiny amount of actual maror but drowns it with lettuce and haroset. The husband, being a manly man alpha male big shot only takes the good stuff. He turns the colors of Joseph's amazing technicolor dreamcoat, but, thankfully, recovers.]

---

179 *Titus Andronicus*, Act 2, Scene 3.

כּוֹרֵךְ

כל אחד מהמסבים לוקח כזית מן המצה השלישית עם כזית מרור,
כורכים יחד, אוכלים בהסבה ובלי ברכה. לפני אכלו אומר:

זֵכֶר לְמִקְדָּשׁ כְּהִלֵּל. כֵּן עָשָׂה הִלֵּל בִּזְמַן שֶׁבֵּית
הַמִּקְדָּשׁ הָיָה קַיָּם.

הָיָה כּוֹרֵךְ מַצָּה וּמָרוֹר וְאוֹכֵל בְּיַחַד, לְקַיֵּם מַה
שֶׁנֶּאֱמַר: xlv עַל מַצּוֹת וּמְרוֹרִים יֹאכְלֻהוּ.

*[לא מספיק שישרוולי הבעל מכוסים במיץ ענבים. כעת ברכיו מכוסים
במיץ מרור וחרוסת (טָעִים מְאוֹד). זה מה שאתה מקבל על הישענות לאחור,
כאשר ההלכה אומרת במפורש להישען שמאלה.]*

---

xlv *Exodus 12:15.*

What Dost Thou Wrap and Fumble in Thine Arms[180]

All present should taketh an olive's measure from the third whole unleavened bread with an olive's measure of bitter greens, wrap them together and consume them while reclining and without saying a blessing. Ere he consumeth it, he should sayeth:

In memory of the Lord's anointed Temple[181] according to Hillel. This is what Hillel would doeth at which hour the Temple much surpassing[182] existed.

He would wrap the unleavened bread and bitter greens and consume them together, in order to fulfill what is stated, "Thou shouldst consume it upon unleavened breads and bitter greens."

[It's not enough the husband's sleeves are covered in grape juice. Now his lap is covered in maror and haroset juice (yum). That's what you get for leaning back when the rules specifically say you lean to the left.]

---

180   *Titus Andronicus*, Act 4, Scene 2.

181   *Macbeth*, Act 2, Scene 3.

182   *The Winter's Tale*, Act 3, Scene 1.

שֻׁלְחָן עוֹרֵךְ

אוכלים ושותים.

[הבעל שמח להשתתף סוף סוף בשיחות. הארוחה הטעימה נטרפת מכל
הלב. הבנים הצעירים כבר נמצאים בלֶג, אבל מוכנים לסחיטה באפיקומן.]

The Set Table Full of Welcome[183]

We strive mightily, but eat and drink as friends.[184]

[The husband is happy to finally participate in the conversations. The delicious meal is devoured heartily. The youngest sons are already in PJs but ready for afikoman blackmail.]

---

183 *The Comedy of Errors*, Act 3, Scene 1.
184 *The Taming of the Shrew*, Act 1, Scene 2.

צָפוּן

[האפיקומן נרכש בעקבות סחיטה מוצלחת של חסכונות החיים של ההורים, שבעצמה באה בעקבות מצוד אחר האפיקומן לאחר שהצעיר הזיז אותו ממקום מחבואו, אך נרדם.]

אחר גמר הסעודה לוקח כל אחד מהמסבים כזית מהמצה שהייתה צפונה לאפיקומן ואוכל ממנה כזית בהסבה. וצריך לאוכלה קודם חצות הלילה.

לפני אכילת האפיקומן יאמר:

זֵכֶר לְקָרְבָּן פֶּסַח הַנֶּאֱכָל עַל הַשּׂוֹבַע.

Hitherto Concealed This[185]

[The afikoman is procured following a successful blackmailing of the parents' life-savings, which itself follows a manhunt for the afikoman after the young one moved it from its hiding spot, but fell asleep.]

After the end of the meal, all those present taketh an olive's measure from the unleavened bread, that wast concealed for the afikoman, and consume an olive's measure from it while reclining.

Before eating the afikoman, he should sayeth:

"In memory of the Passover sacrifice that wast eaten upon being satiated."

---

185 *Hamlet*, Act I, Scene 2.

בֵּרֵךְ

God Bless You, Sir![186]

—

ACT III

---

186 *Hamlet*, Act 3, Scene 2.

בִּרְכַּת הַמָּזוֹן

מוזגים כוס שלישי ומברכים בִּרְכַּת המזון.

שִׁיר הַמַּעֲלוֹת, בְּשׁוּב ה' אֶת שִׁיבַת צִיּוֹן הָיִינוּ כְּחֹלְמִים. אָז יִמָּלֵא שְׂחוֹק פִּינוּ וּלְשׁוֹנֵנוּ רִנָּה. אָז יֹאמְרוּ בַגּוֹיִם: הִגְדִּיל ה' לַעֲשׂוֹת עִם אֵלֶּה. הִגְדִּיל ה' לַעֲשׂוֹת עִמָּנוּ, הָיִינוּ שְׂמֵחִים. שׁוּבָה ה' אֶת שְׁבִיתֵנוּ כַּאֲפִיקִים בַּנֶּגֶב. הַזֹּרְעִים בְּדִמְעָה, בְּרִנָּה יִקְצֹרוּ. הָלוֹךְ יֵלֵךְ וּבָכֹה נֹשֵׂא מֶשֶׁךְ הַזָּרַע, בֹּא יָבֹא בְרִנָּה נֹשֵׂא אֲלֻמֹּתָיו[xlvi].

שלושה שֶׁאָכְלוּ כְּאֶחָד חיבים לזמן והמזַמן פותח:

רַבּוֹתַי נְבָרֵךְ:

המסבים עונים:

יְהִי שֵׁם ה' מְבֹרָךְ מֵעַתָּה וְעַד עוֹלָם[xlvii].

[xlvi] Psalms 126.
[xlvii] *Psalms* 113:2.

Grace After Meals

We poureth the third cup and recite the Grace over the food.

A Song of Ascents; at which hour the Lord wilt bringeth back the captivity of Zion, we wilt beest like such stuff as dreams are made on.[187] Then our mouth wilt beest replete with mirth and joy[188] and our tongue joyful sound of sweetest melody;[189] then they wilt sayeth among the nations; "The Lord hath done greatly with these." The Lord hath done most wondrous things with us; we art joyous. Lord, returneth our captivity like streams in the desert. Those that sow with tears of innocency and terms of zeal,[190] wilt reap with joyful song. He who surely goeth and cries, he carryeth the measure of seed, he wilt surely cometh in joyful song and carryeth his sheaves.

Three that consumed together art obligated to introduce the blessing and the vaward of the introduction openeth as follows:

Mine masters, alloweth us bless:

All those present answer:

May the Name of the Lord beest blessed from now and still.

---

187   *The Tempest*, Act 4, Scene 1.
188   *Henry VI*, Part I, Act 1, Scene 6.
189   *Henry IV*, Part II, Act 3, Scene 1.
190   *Henry IV*, Part I, Act 4, Scene 3.

הַמְזַמֵּן אוֹמֵר:

בִּרְשׁוּת מָרָנָן וְרַבָּנָן וְרַבּוֹתַי, נְבָרֵךְ [אֱלֹהֵינוּ] שֶׁאָכַלְנוּ מִשֶּׁלּוֹ.

הַמְסֻבִּים עוֹנִים:

בָּרוּךְ [אֱלֹהֵינוּ] שֶׁאָכַלְנוּ מִשֶּׁלּוֹ וּבְטוּבוֹ חָיִינוּ.

הַמְזַמֵּן חוֹזֵר וְאוֹמֵר.

בָּרוּךְ [אֱלֹהֵינוּ] שֶׁאָכַלְנוּ מִשֶּׁלּוֹ וּבְטוּבוֹ חָיִינוּ.

כֻּלָּם אוֹמְרִים:

בָּרוּךְ אַתָּה ה', אֱלֹהֵינוּ מֶלֶךְ הָעוֹלָם, הַזָּן אֶת הָעוֹלָם כֻּלּוֹ בְּטוּבוֹ בְּחֵן בְּחֶסֶד וּבְרַחֲמִים, הוּא נוֹתֵן לֶחֶם לְכָל בָּשָׂר כִּי לְעוֹלָם חַסְדּוֹ. וּבְטוּבוֹ הַגָּדוֹל תָּמִיד לֹא חָסַר לָנוּ, וְאַל יֶחְסַר לָנוּ מָזוֹן לְעוֹלָם וָעֶד. בַּעֲבוּר שְׁמוֹ הַגָּדוֹל, כִּי הוּא אֵל זָן וּמְפַרְנֵס לַכֹּל וּמֵטִיב לַכֹּל, וּמֵכִין מָזוֹן לְכָל בְּרִיּוֹתָיו אֲשֶׁר בָּרָא. בָּרוּךְ אַתָּה ה', הַזָּן אֶת הַכֹּל.

The vaward sayeth:

With the permission of our gentlemen and our teachers, my masters and my common friends,[191] alloweth us bless [our God] from whom we hast eaten.

Those present answer:

Blessed is [our God] from whom we hast eaten and from whose goodness we liveth.

The vaward repeats and sayeth:

Blessed is [our God] from whom we hast eaten and from whose goodness we liveth.

They all sayeth:

Blessed art thee, Lord our God, King of the universe, who nourishes the entire world in His goodness, in grace, in kindness, and in mercy; He giveth bread to all flesh since His kindness is still. And in His most wondrous goodness, we at each moment hast not lacked, and may we not want nourishment still and at each moment, because of His most wondrous name. Since He is a power that feeds and provides for all and doest good to all and prepares nourishment for all of His creatures that He hath made. Blessed art thee, Lord, who sustaineth all.

---

191 *Coriolanus*, Act 3, Scene 3.

נוֹדֶה לְּךָ ה' אֱלֹהֵינוּ עַל שֶׁהִנְחַלְתָּ לַאֲבוֹתֵינוּ אֶרֶץ חֶמְדָּה טוֹבָה וּרְחָבָה, וְעַל שֶׁהוֹצֵאתָנוּ ה' אֱלֹהֵינוּ מֵאֶרֶץ מִצְרַיִם, וּפְדִיתָנוּ מִבֵּית עֲבָדִים, וְעַל בְּרִיתְךָ שֶׁחָתַמְתָּ בִּבְשָׂרֵנוּ, וְעַל תּוֹרָתְךָ שֶׁלִּמַּדְתָּנוּ, וְעַל חֻקֶּיךָ שֶׁהוֹדַעְתָּנוּ, וְעַל חַיִּים חֵן וָחֶסֶד שֶׁחוֹנַנְתָּנוּ, וְעַל אֲכִילַת מָזוֹן שֶׁאַתָּה זָן וּמְפַרְנֵס אוֹתָנוּ תָּמִיד, בְּכָל יוֹם וּבְכָל עֵת וּבְכָל שָׁעָה.

וְעַל הַכֹּל ה' אֱלֹהֵינוּ, אֲנַחְנוּ מוֹדִים לָךְ וּמְבָרְכִים אוֹתָךְ, יִתְבָּרַךְ שִׁמְךָ בְּפִי כָּל חַי תָּמִיד לְעוֹלָם וָעֶד. כַּכָּתוּב:[xlviii] וְאָכַלְתָּ וְשָׂבַעְתָּ וּבֵרַכְתָּ אֶת ה' אֱלֹהֶיךָ עַל הָאָרֶץ הַטּוֹבָה אֲשֶׁר נָתַן לָךְ. בָּרוּךְ אַתָּה ה', עַל הָאָרֶץ וְעַל הַמָּזוֹן.

[xlviii] Deuteronomy 8:10.

We thank Thee, Lord our God, that thou hast given as an inheritance to our ancestors a lovely, valorous and broad land, and that thee tooketh us out, Lord our God, from the land of Egypt and that Thee redeemed us from a house of slaves, and for Thy covenant which Thou hast sealed in our flesh, and for Thy Torah that Thou hast taught us, and for the rigour of the statutes[192] which thou hast madeth known to us, and for life, grace and kindness that thou hast granted us and for the eating of the food and nourishment[193] that Thee feedeth and provideth for us at each moment, on all days in the year,[194] and at all times alike[195] and every hour.[196]

And for everything, Lord our God, we thank Thee and bless Thee; may Thy name beest blessed by the mouth of all life, constantly still and at each moment, as tis writ,[197] "And thee shalt consume and thee shalt beest satiated and thee shalt bless the Lord thy God for the good land that He hath given thee." Blessed art Thee, Lord, for the land and for the nourishment.

192   *Measure for Measure*, Act 1, Scene 4.
193   *The Two Noble Kinsmen*, Act 2, Scene 1.
194   *Romeo and Juliet*, Act 1, Scene 3.
195   *Timon of Athens*, Act 5, Scene 1.
196   *Antony and Cleopatra*, Act 1, Scene 4.
197   *The Comedy of Errors*, Act 4, Scene 3.

רַחֵם נָא ה' אֱלֹהֵינוּ עַל יִשְׂרָאֵל עַמֶּךָ וְעַל יְרוּשָׁלַיִם
עִירֶךָ וְעַל צִיּוֹן מִשְׁכַּן כְּבוֹדֶךָ וְעַל מַלְכוּת בֵּית דָּוִד
מְשִׁיחֶךָ וְעַל הַבַּיִת הַגָּדוֹל וְהַקָּדוֹשׁ שֶׁנִּקְרָא שִׁמְךָ
עָלָיו: אֱלֹהֵינוּ אָבִינוּ, רְעֵנוּ זוּנֵנוּ פַּרְנְסֵנוּ וְכַלְכְּלֵנוּ
וְהַרְוִיחֵנוּ, וְהַרְוַח לָנוּ ה' אֱלֹהֵינוּ מְהֵרָה מִכָּל
צָרוֹתֵינוּ. וְנָא אַל תַּצְרִיכֵנוּ ה' אֱלֹהֵינוּ, לֹא לִידֵי
מַתְּנַת בָּשָׂר וָדָם וְלֹא לִידֵי הַלְוָאתָם, כִּי אִם לְיָדְךָ
הַמְּלֵאָה הַפְּתוּחָה הַקְּדוֹשָׁה וְהָרְחָבָה, שֶׁלֹּא נֵבוֹשׁ
וְלֹא נִכָּלֵם לְעוֹלָם וָעֶד.

Please hast mercy, Lord our God, upon Israel, of thy people[198]; and upon Jerusalem, thy city and upon Zion, the place of Thy dwelling[199] of Thy glory; and upon the monarchy of the House of David, thy appointed one; and upon the most wondrous and holy house that Thy name hath called upon. Our God, our Father, tend us, sustain us, provide for us, relieve us, and giveth us quick relief, Lord our God, from all of our troubles. And please doth not maketh us needy, Lord our God, not for the gifts of flesh and blood,[200] and not for their loans, but rather from thy full, ope, holy and broad hand, so that we not beest embarrassed and we not beest ashamed[201] still and at each moment.

---

198   *Henry V*, Act 3, Scene 3.
199   *The Winter's Tale*, Act 4, Scene 4.
200   *The Tempest*, Act 5, Scene 1.
201   *The Merchant of Venice*, Act 2, Scene 3.

רְצֵה וְהַחֲלִיצֵנוּ ה' אֱלֹהֵינוּ בְּמִצְוֹתֶיךָ וּבְמִצְוַת יוֹם הַשְּׁבִיעִי הַשַּׁבָּת הַגָּדוֹל וְהַקָּדוֹשׁ הַזֶּה. כִּי יוֹם זֶה גָּדוֹל וְקָדוֹשׁ הוּא לְפָנֶיךָ לִשְׁבָּת בּוֹ וְלָנוּחַ בּוֹ בְּאַהֲבָה כְּמִצְוַת רְצוֹנֶךָ. וּבִרְצוֹנְךָ הָנִיחַ לָנוּ ה' אֱלֹהֵינוּ שֶׁלֹּא תְהֵא צָרָה וְיָגוֹן וַאֲנָחָה בְּיוֹם מְנוּחָתֵנוּ. וְהַרְאֵנוּ ה' אֱלֹהֵינוּ בְּנֶחָמַת צִיּוֹן עִירֶךָ וּבְבִנְיַן יְרוּשָׁלַיִם עִיר קָדְשֶׁךָ כִּי אַתָּה הוּא בַּעַל הַיְשׁוּעוֹת וּבַעַל הַנֶּחָמוֹת.

On Sabbath, we addeth the following paragraph:

May thee beest pleased withal[202] to embolden us, Lord our God, in thy commandments and in the command of the seventh day, of this most wondrous and holy Shabbat, since this day is most wondrous and holy ere thee, to ceaseth work upon it and to rest so hung upon with love,[203] according to the commandment of thy will.[204] And with thy will, allow us as we prove,[205] Lord our God, that we should not hast trouble, and grief and woe[206] and sighing like furnace, with a woeful ballad[207] on the day of our rest. And may Thee showeth us, Lord our God, this grief is crowned with consolation[208] of Zion, thy city and the building of Jerusalem, thy holy city; since thee art the Master of salvations and the Master of consolations.

202 *The Two Gentlemen of Verona*, Act 2, Scene 7.

203 *A Midsummer Night's Dream*, Act 3, Scene 2.

204 *The Comedy of Errors*, Act 2, Scene 1.

205 *Troilus and Cressida*, Act 3, Scene 2.

206 *Henry VI, Part III*, Act 2, Scene 5.

207 *As You Like It*, Act 2, Scene 7.

208 *Antony and Cleopatra*, Act 1, Scene 2.

אֱלֹהֵינוּ וֵאלֹהֵי אֲבוֹתֵינוּ, יַעֲלֶה וְיָבֹא וְיַגִּיעַ וְיֵרָאֶה
וְיֵרָצֶה וְיִשָּׁמַע וְיִפָּקֵד וְיִזָּכֵר זִכְרוֹנֵנוּ וּפִקְדוֹנֵנוּ,
וְזִכְרוֹן אֲבוֹתֵינוּ, וְזִכְרוֹן מָשִׁיחַ בֶּן דָּוִד עַבְדֶּךָ,
וְזִכְרוֹן יְרוּשָׁלַיִם עִיר קָדְשֶׁךָ, וְזִכְרוֹן כָּל עַמְּךָ בֵּית
יִשְׂרָאֵל לְפָנֶיךָ, לִפְלֵיטָה לְטוֹבָה לְחֵן וּלְחֶסֶד
וּלְרַחֲמִים, לְחַיִּים וּלְשָׁלוֹם בְּיוֹם חַג הַמַּצּוֹת הַזֶּה
זָכְרֵנוּ ה' אֱלֹהֵינוּ בּוֹ לְטוֹבָה וּפָקְדֵנוּ בּוֹ לִבְרָכָה
וְהוֹשִׁיעֵנוּ בּוֹ לְחַיִּים. וּבִדְבַר יְשׁוּעָה וְרַחֲמִים חוּס
וְחָנֵּנוּ וְרַחֵם עָלֵינוּ וְהוֹשִׁיעֵנוּ, כִּי אֵלֶיךָ עֵינֵינוּ, כִּי
אֵל מֶלֶךְ חַנּוּן וְרַחוּם אָתָּה. וּבְנֵה יְרוּשָׁלַיִם עִיר
הַקֹּדֶשׁ בִּמְהֵרָה בְיָמֵינוּ. בָּרוּךְ אַתָּה ה', בּוֹנֵה
בְרַחֲמָיו יְרוּשָׁלַיִם. אָמֵן.

God and God of our ancestors, may thither ascend and cometh and reacheth and beest seen and beest acceptable and beest heard and beest recalled and beest recalled our remembrance and our recollection and the remembrance of our ancestors and the remembrance of the messiah, the son of David, thy servant; and the remembrance of Jerusalem, thy holy city; and the remembrance of all thy people, the house of Israel in front of thee, for survival, for good, for grace, and for kindness, and for mercy, for life and for peace on this day of the Festival of Unleavened Breads, recall us, Lord our God, on it for good and recall us on it for survival and save us on it for life, and by the word of salvation and mercy, pity and grace us and hast mercy on us and save us, since our eyes art upon Thee, since Thee art a graceful and merciful Power. And may Thee buildeth Jerusalem, the holy city, apace and in our days. Blessed art Thee, Lord, who buildeth Jerusalem in His mercy. Amen. So fall to it.[209]

---

209 *Timon of Athens*, Act I, Scene 2.

בָּרוּךְ אַתָּה ה', אֱלֹהֵינוּ מֶלֶךְ הָעוֹלָם, הָאֵל אָבִינוּ
מַלְכֵּנוּ אַדִירֵנוּ בּוֹרְאֵנוּ גּוֹאֲלֵנוּ יוֹצְרֵנוּ קְדוֹשֵׁנוּ
קְדוֹשׁ יַעֲקֹב רוֹעֵנוּ רוֹעֵה יִשְׂרָאֵל הַמֶּלֶךְ הַטּוֹב
וְהַמֵּטִיב לַכֹּל שֶׁבְּכָל יוֹם וָיוֹם הוּא הֵטִיב, הוּא
מֵטִיב, הוּא יֵיטִיב לָנוּ. הוּא גְמָלָנוּ הוּא גוֹמְלֵנוּ הוּא
יִגְמְלֵנוּ לָעַד, לְחֵן וּלְחֶסֶד וּלְרַחֲמִים וּלְרֶוַח הַצָּלָה
וְהַצְלָחָה, בְּרָכָה וִישׁוּעָה נֶחָמָה פַּרְנָסָה וְכַלְכָּלָה
וְרַחֲמִים וְחַיִּים וְשָׁלוֹם וְכָל טוֹב, וּמִכָּל טוּב לְעוֹלָם
עַל יְחַסְּרֵנוּ.

Blessed art thee, Lord our God, King of the universe, the Power, our Father, our King, our Mighty One,[210] our Creator, our Redeemer, our Shaper, our Holy One, the Holy One of Ya'akov, our Shepherd, the Shepherd of the flock[211] of Israel, the valorous King, who doest good to all, since on every single day he hath done good, He doest valorous, He shalt perchance doeth good,[212] to us He hath granted us, He grants us, He wilt grant us still in grace and in kindness, and in mercy, and in relief rescue and success, blessing and salvation, consolation, provision and relief and mercy and life and peace and all good; and may we not want any good ever.

210   *The Two Noble Kinsmen*, Act 5, Scene 1.
211   *Henry VI*, Part II, Act 2, Scene 2.
212   *King Lear*, Act 5, Scene 3.

הָרַחֲמָן הוּא יִמְלוֹךְ עָלֵינוּ לְעוֹלָם וָעֶד. הָרַחֲמָן הוּא
יִתְבָּרַךְ בַּשָּׁמַיִם וּבָאָרֶץ. הָרַחֲמָן הוּא יִשְׁתַּבַּח לְדוֹר
דוֹרִים, וְיִתְפָּאַר בָּנוּ לָעַד וּלְנֵצַח נְצָחִים, וְיִתְהַדַּר
בָּנוּ לָעַד וּלְעוֹלְמֵי עוֹלָמִים. הָרַחֲמָן הוּא יְפַרְנְסֵנוּ
בְּכָבוֹד. הָרַחֲמָן הוּא יִשְׁבּוֹר עֻלֵּנוּ מֵעַל צַוָּארֵנוּ,
וְהוּא יוֹלִיכֵנוּ קוֹמְמִיּוּת לְאַרְצֵנוּ. הָרַחֲמָן הוּא יִשְׁלַח
לָנוּ בְּרָכָה מְרֻבָּה בַּבַּיִת הַזֶּה, וְעַל שֻׁלְחָן זֶה
שֶׁאָכַלְנוּ עָלָיו. הָרַחֲמָן הוּא יִשְׁלַח לָנוּ אֶת אֵלִיָּהוּ
הַנָּבִיא זָכוּר לַטּוֹב, וִיבַשֶּׂר לָנוּ בְּשׂוֹרוֹת טוֹבוֹת
יְשׁוּעוֹת וְנֶחָמוֹת.

הָרַחֲמָן הוּא יְבָרֵךְ אֶת בַּעֲלִי / אִשְׁתִּי. הָרַחֲמָן הוּא
יְבָרֵךְ אֶת [אָבִי מוֹרִי] בַּעַל הַבַּיִת הַזֶּה. וְאֶת [אִמִּי
מוֹרָתִי] בַּעֲלַת הַבַּיִת הַזֶּה, אוֹתָם וְאֶת בֵּיתָם וְאֶת
זַרְעָם וְאֶת כָּל אֲשֶׁר לָהֶם. אוֹתָנוּ וְאֶת כָּל אֲשֶׁר
לָנוּ, כְּמוֹ שֶׁנִּתְבָּרְכוּ אֲבוֹתֵינוּ אַבְרָהָם יִצְחָק וְיַעֲקֹב
בַּכֹּל מִכֹּל כֹּל, כֵּן יְבָרֵךְ אוֹתָנוּ כֻּלָּנוּ יַחַד בִּבְרָכָה
שְׁלֵמָה, וְנֹאמַר, אָמֵן.

May the Merciful One reigneth over us still and at each moment. May the Merciful One beest blessed in the heavens and earth.[213] May the Merciful One beest praised for all generations, and exalted among us still and ever, and glorified among us at each moment and infinitely for all infinities. May the Merciful One sustain us honorably. May the Merciful One shaketh off our slavish yoke[214] from upon our necks and bringeth us as upright as the cedar[215] to our land. May the Merciful One sendeth us multiple blessings, to this home and upon this table upon which we hast eaten. May the Merciful One sendeth us Eliyahu the prophet, may he beest recalled for good, and he shalt announceth to us tidings of good, of salvation and of consolation.

May the Merciful One bless mine husband![216] my queen, my life, my wife.[217] May the Merciful One bless]O my father,[218] mine teacher[, the master of this home and [O my mother,[219] mine teacher[, the mistress of the house,[220] they and their home and their offspring and everything that is theirs. Us and all that is ours as wast blessed Avraham, Yitschak, and Ya'akov, in everything, from everything, with everything, so too should He bless us, all of us together, with a complete blessing and we shalt sayeth Amen to all.[221]

213 *Antony and Cleopatra*, Act 3, Scene 12.

214 *Richard II*, Act 2, Scene 1.

215 *Love's Labour's Lost*, Act 4, Scene 3.

216 *Othello*, Act 5, Scene 2.

217 *Cymbeline*, Act 5, Scene 5.

218 *The Tempest*, Act 3, Scene 1.

219 *Coriolanus*, Act 5, Scene 3.

220 *The Merchant of Venice*, Act 5, Scene 1.

221 *Richard III*, Act 5, Scene 5.

בַּמָּרוֹם יְלַמְּדוּ עֲלֵיהֶם וְעָלֵינוּ זְכוּת שֶׁתְּהֵא לְמִשְׁמֶרֶת שָׁלוֹם. וְנִשָּׂא בְרָכָה מֵאֵת ה', וּצְדָקָה מֵאלֹהֵי יִשְׁעֵנוּ, וְנִמְצָא חֵן וְשֵׂכֶל טוֹב בְּעֵינֵי אֱלֹהִים וְאָדָם.

בשבת: הָרַחֲמָן הוּא יַנְחִילֵנוּ יוֹם שֶׁכֻּלּוֹ שַׁבָּת וּמְנוּחָה לְחַיֵּי הָעוֹלָמִים. הָרַחֲמָן הוּא יַנְחִילֵנוּ יוֹם שֶׁכֻּלּוֹ טוֹב.

הָרַחֲמָן הוּא יְזַכֵּנוּ לִימוֹת הַמָּשִׁיחַ וּלְחַיֵּי הָעוֹלָם הַבָּא. מִגְדּוֹל יְשׁוּעוֹת מַלְכּוֹ וְעֹשֶׂה חֶסֶד לִמְשִׁיחוֹ לְדָוִד וּלְזַרְעוֹ עַד עוֹלָם.[xlix] עֹשֶׂה שָׁלוֹם בִּמְרוֹמָיו, הוּא יַעֲשֶׂה שָׁלוֹם עָלֵינוּ וְעַל כָּל יִשְׂרָאֵל וְאִמְרוּ, אָמֵן.

יְראוּ אֶת ה' קְדֹשָׁיו, כִּי אֵין מַחְסוֹר לִירֵאָיו. כְּפִירִים רָשׁוּ וְרָעֵבוּ, וְדֹרְשֵׁי ה' לֹא יַחְסְרוּ כָל טוֹב.[l] הוֹדוּ לַיי כִּי טוֹב כִּי לְעוֹלָם חַסְדּוֹ.[li] פּוֹתֵחַ אֶת יָדֶךָ, וּמַשְׂבִּיעַ לְכָל חַי רָצוֹן.[lii] בָּרוּךְ הַגֶּבֶר אֲשֶׁר יִבְטַח בַּיי, וְהָיָה ה' מִבְטַחוֹ.[liii] נַעַר הָיִיתִי גַּם זָקַנְתִּי, וְלֹא רָאִיתִי צַדִּיק נֶעֱזָב, וְזַרְעוֹ מְבַקֶּשׁ לָחֶם.[liv] ה' עֹז לְעַמּוֹ יִתֵּן, ה' יְבָרֵךְ אֶת עַמּוֹ בַשָּׁלוֹם.[lv]

[xlix] *II Samuel* 22:51.
[l] *Psalms* 34:10-11.
[li] *Ibid* 118:1.
[lii] *Ibid* 146:16.
[liii] *Jeremiah* 17:7.
[liv] *Psalms* 37:25.
[lv] *Ibid* 29:11.

From above, may they advocate upon them and upon our merit, that should protect us in peace; and may we carryeth a blessing from the Lord and charity from the God of our salvation; and findeth grace and good understanding in the eyes of God and man.[222]

On Shabbat, we say: May the Merciful One give us to inherit the day that will be completely Shabbat and rest in everlasting life. May the Merciful One give us to inherit the day that will be all good.

May the Merciful One giveth us merit for the times of the messiah and for life in the world to come.[223] A tower of strength[224] and salvation is our King; may He doeth kindness with his messiah, with David and his offspring, still. The One who maketh peace above, may He maketh peace upon us and upon all of Israel; and grace sayeth Amen to it![225]

Fear the Lord, His holy ones, since thither is no lacking for those that fear Him. Young lions may wend without hunger, but those that seek the Lord wilt not want any good thing. Thank the Lord, since He is good, since His kindness is still. Thee ope thy hand and satisfy the wilt of all living things. Blessed is the sir that trusts in the Lord and the Lord is his security. I wast a youth and I hast eke aged and I hast not seen a righteous sir forsaken and his offspring seeking bread. The Lord wilt giveth courage to His people. The Lord wilt bless His people with peace.

222 *Henry VI, Part III*, Act 1, Scene 3.
223 *Troilus and Cressida*, Act 3, Scene 2.
224 *Richard III*, Act 5, Scene 3.
225 *Much Ado About Nothing*, Act 2, Scene 1.

כּוֹס שְׁלִישִׁי

בָּרוּךְ אַתָּה ה', אֱלֹהֵינוּ מֶלֶךְ הָעוֹלָם בּוֹרֵא פְּרִי הַגָּפֶן.

ושותים בהסיבה ואינו מברך ברכה אחרונה.

Third Flagon of Wine Be A Poured[226]

Blessed art thee, Lord our God, King of the universe, who maketh the fruit of the vine.

We drinketh while reclining and doeth not sayeth a blessing afterwards.

---

226 *Hamlet*, Act 5, Scene 1.

שְׁפֹךְ חֲמָתְךָ

מוזגים כוס של אליהו ופותחים את הדלת.

[אליהו נכנס.]

שְׁפֹךְ חֲמָתְךָ אֶל־הַגּוֹיִם אֲשֶׁר לֹא יְדָעוּךָ וְעַל־
מַמְלָכוֹת אֲשֶׁר בְּשִׁמְךָ לֹא קָרָאוּ. כִּי אָכַל אֶת־יַעֲקֹב
וְאֶת־נָוֵהוּ הֵשַׁמּוּ. [lvi] שְׁפֹךְ־עֲלֵיהֶם זַעֲמֶךָ וַחֲרוֹן אַפְּךָ
יַשִּׂיגֵם. [lvii] תִּרְדֹּף בְּאַף וְתַשְׁמִידֵם מִתַּחַת שְׁמֵי ה'. [lviii]

[אליהו יוצא.]

[lvi] *Psalms* 79:67.
[lvii] *Ibid* 69:25.
[lviii] Lamentations 3:66.

Poureth Out Thy Wrath

We poureth the cup of Eliyahu and ope the door.[227]

[Elijah enters.]

Poureth out thy wrath upon the nations that didst not knoweth thee and upon the kingdoms and provinces[228] that didst not calleth upon thy Name! Since they hast consumed Yaakov and laid waste his habitation. Poureth out thy fury upon them and the fierceness of thy snuffs shalt reacheth them! Thee shalt pursue them with snuffs and eradicate them from under the skies of the Lord.

[Elijah exits.]

---

227 *The Comedy of Errors*, Act 3, Scene 1.
228 *Antony and Cleopatra*, Act 3, Scene 10.

הַלֵּל

Praise You While I Have a Stomach[229]

—

ACT IV

229   *The Merchant of Venice*, Act 3, Scene 5.

מַחֲצִית הַשְּׁנִיָּה שֶׁל הַהַלֵּל

[הבעל שוב ממשיך, כשהשולחן מתפנה, והמחותנים והאורחים
מתווכחים על פוליטיקה או משהו.]

מוזגין כוס רביעי וגומרין עליו את ההלל.

לֹא לָנוּ, ה', לֹא לָנוּ, כִּי לְשִׁמְךָ תֵּן כָּבוֹד, עַל חַסְדְּךָ
עַל אֲמִתֶּךָ. לָמָּה יֹאמְרוּ הַגּוֹיִם אַיֵּה נָא אֱלֹהֵיהֶם.
וֵאלֹהֵינוּ בַשָּׁמַיִם, כֹּל אֲשֶׁר חָפֵץ עָשָׂה. עֲצַבֵּיהֶם
כֶּסֶף וְזָהָב מַעֲשֵׂה יְדֵי אָדָם. פֶּה לָהֶם וְלֹא יְדַבֵּרוּ,
עֵינַיִם לָהֶם וְלֹא יִרְאוּ. אָזְנַיִם לָהֶם וְלֹא יִשְׁמָעוּ, אַף
לָהֶם וְלֹא יְרִיחוּן. יְדֵיהֶם וְלֹא יְמִישׁוּן, רַגְלֵיהֶם וְלֹא
יְהַלֵּכוּ, לֹא יֶהְגּוּ בִּגְרוֹנָם. כְּמוֹהֶם יִהְיוּ עֹשֵׂיהֶם, כֹּל
אֲשֶׁר בֹּטֵחַ בָּהֶם. יִשְׂרָאֵל בְּטַח בַּיי, עֶזְרָם וּמָגִנָּם
הוּא. בֵּית אַהֲרֹן בִּטְחוּ בַּיי, עֶזְרָם וּמָגִנָּם הוּא. יִרְאֵי
ה' בִּטְחוּ בַּיי, עֶזְרָם וּמָגִנָּם הוּא.^{lix}

---

lix *Psalms* 15:1-11

Second Half of Praise

[The husband commences with motoring again, as the table is cleared, and the in-laws and guests argue over politics or something.]

We poureth the fourth cup and completeth the praise.

Not to us, not to us, but rather to thy name, giveth glory for thy kindness and for thy truth. wherefore should the nations sayeth, "Say, whither is their God?" But our God is in the heavens, all that He wanted, He hath done. Their idols art silver and gold, the work of men's hands. They have a mouth but doeth not speaketh; they have eyes but doeth not see. They have ears but doeth not heareth; they have a nose but doeth not smelleth. Hands, but they doeth not feeleth; feet, but doeth not walketh; they doeth not maketh a peep from their throat. Like they wilt beest their makers, all those that trust in them. Israel, trust in the Lord; their help and sword and shield[230] is He. House of Aharon, trust in the Lord; their help a lance, and a shield[231] is He. Those that feareth the Lord, trusteth in the Lord; their help and shield afore your heart[232] is He.

---

230 *Henry V*, Act 3, Scene 2.
231 *King Edward III*, Act 3, Scene 3.
232 *The Two Noble Kinsmen*, Act I, Scene I.

יי זְכָרָנוּ יְבָרֵךְ. יְבָרֵךְ אֶת בֵּית יִשְׂרָאֵל, יְבָרֵךְ אֶת
בֵּית אַהֲרֹן, יְבָרֵךְ יִרְאֵי ה', הַקְּטַנִּים עִם הַגְּדֹלִים.
יֹסֵף ה' עֲלֵיכֶם, עֲלֵיכֶם וְעַל בְּנֵיכֶם. בְּרוּכִים אַתֶּם
לַיָי, עֹשֵׂה שָׁמַיִם וָאָרֶץ. הַשָּׁמַיִם שָׁמַיִם לַיָי וְהָאָרֶץ
נָתַן לִבְנֵי אָדָם. לֹא הַמֵּתִים יְהַלְלוּ יָהּ וְלֹא כָּל יֹרְדֵי
דוּמָה. וַאֲנַחְנוּ נְבָרֵךְ יָהּ מֵעַתָּה וְעַד עוֹלָם.
הַלְלוּיָהּ[lx].

אָהַבְתִּי כִּי יִשְׁמַע ה' אֶת קוֹלִי תַּחֲנוּנָי. כִּי הִטָּה אָזְנוֹ
לִי וּבְיָמַי אֶקְרָא. אֲפָפוּנִי חֶבְלֵי מָוֶת וּמְצָרֵי שְׁאוֹל
מְצָאוּנִי, צָרָה וְיָגוֹן אֶמְצָא. וּבְשֵׁם ה' אֶקְרָא: אָנָּא
ה' מַלְּטָה נַפְשִׁי. חַנּוּן ה' וְצַדִּיק, וֵאלֹהֵינוּ מְרַחֵם.
שֹׁמֵר פְּתָאיִם ה', דַּלּוֹתִי וְלִי יְהוֹשִׁיעַ. שׁוּבִי נַפְשִׁי
לִמְנוּחָיְכִי, כִּי ה' גָּמַל עָלָיְכִי. כִּי חִלַּצְתָּ נַפְשִׁי
מִמָּוֶת, אֶת עֵינִי מִן דִּמְעָה, אֶת רַגְלִי מִדֶּחִי. אֶתְהַלֵּךְ
לִפְנֵי ה' בְּאַרְצוֹת הַחַיִּים. הֶאֱמַנְתִּי כִּי אֲדַבֵּר, אֲנִי
עָנִיתִי מְאֹד. אֲנִי אָמַרְתִּי בְחָפְזִי כָּל הָאָדָם כֹּזֵב[lxi].

lx *Psalms* 15:12-18.
lxi *Psalms* 116:1-11.

The Lord who recalls us, wilt blesseth; He wilt blesseth the House of Israel; He wilt blesseth the House of Aharon. He wilt blesseth those that fear the Lord, the small ones with the most wondrous ones. May the Lord bringeth increase to thee, to thee and to thy children. Blessed art thee to the Lord, the maker of the heavens and the earth. O the heavens,[233] art the Lord's heavens, but the earth he hath given to the children of man. Tis not the dead that wilt praise the Lord, and not those that wend down to silence that.[234] But we wilt blesseth the Lord from now and still. Halleluyah!

I hast loved the Lord since He doeth hear mine voice, mine supplications. Since He inclined His ear to me, and in mine days, I wilt calleth out. The pangs of death[235] hast encircled me and the straits of the Pit hath found me and I hath found grief. And in the name of the Lord I hath called, "Please Lord, Spare mine life and soul."[236] Gracious is the Lord and righteous, and our God acts mercifully. The Lord gazes over the fartuous; I wast poor and he hath saved me. Returneth, mine soul to thy tranquility, since the Lord hath favored thee. Since thou hast rescued mine soul from death, mine eyes from tears, mine feet from stumbling. I wilt walketh ere the Lord in the lands of the living. I hast trusted, at which hour I speaketh I am very afflicted. I hath said in mine haste, all men art hypocritical.

233 *The Tempest*, Act 1, Scene 2.
234 *Coriolanus*, Act 1, Scene 9.
235 *Twelfth Night*, Act 1, Scene 5.
236 *Henry VI*, Part II, Act 4, Scene 1.

מָה אָשִׁיב לַיי כֹּל תַּגְמוּלוֹהִי עָלָי. כּוֹס יְשׁוּעוֹת
אֶשָּׂא וּבְשֵׁם ה' אֶקְרָא. נְדָרַי לַיי אֲשַׁלֵּם נֶגְדָה נָּא
לְכָל עַמּוֹ. יָקָר בְּעֵינֵי ה' הַמָּוְתָה לַחֲסִידָיו. אָנָּה ה'
כִּי אֲנִי עַבְדֶּךָ, אֲנִי עַבְדְּךָ בֶּן אֲמָתֶךָ, פִּתַּחְתָּ
לְמוֹסֵרָי. לְךָ אֶזְבַּח זֶבַח תּוֹדָה וּבְשֵׁם ה' אֶקְרָא.
נְדָרַי לַיי אֲשַׁלֵּם נֶגְדָה נָּא לְכָל עַמּוֹ. בְּחַצְרוֹת בֵּית
ה', בְּתוֹכֵכִי יְרוּשָׁלָיִם. הַלְלוּיָהּ[lxii].

הַלְלוּ אֶת ה' כָּל גּוֹיִם, שַׁבְּחוּהוּ כָּל הָאֻמִּים. כִּי גָבַר
עָלֵינוּ חַסְדּוֹ, וֶאֱמֶת ה' לְעוֹלָם. הַלְלוּיָהּ. הוֹדוּ לַיי
כִּי טוֹב כִּי לְעוֹלָם חַסְדּוֹ. יֹאמַר נָא יִשְׂרָאֵל כִּי
לְעוֹלָם חַסְדּוֹ. יֹאמְרוּ נָא בֵית אַהֲרֹן כִּי לְעוֹלָם
חַסְדּוֹ. יֹאמְרוּ נָא יִרְאֵי ה' כִּי לְעוֹלָם חַסְדּוֹ[lxiii].

lxii *Psalms* 116:12-19.
lxiii *Psalms* 117-118:4.

What I do beseech you[237] giveth back to the Lord for all that he hath favored me? A cup of salvations I wilt raiseth up and I wilt calleth out in the name of the Lord. Mine vows to the Lord I wilt payeth, now in front of His entire people. Precious in the eyes of the Lord is the death of His pious ones. Please Lord, since I am thy servant, the son of thy maidservant. Thou hast opened mine chains. To thee wilt, I giveth a thanksgiving offering and I wilt calleth out in the name of the Lord. Mine vows to the Lord I wilt payeth, now in front of His entire people. In the courtyards of the house of the Lord, in thy midst, Jerusalem. Halleluyah!

Praise the name of the Lord, all nations; extol Him all peoples. Since His kindness hath overwhelmed all[238] of us and the truth of the Lord is still. Halleluyah! Thank the Lord, since He is good, since His kindness is still. Alloweth Israel now sayeth, "Thank the Lord, since He is good, since His kindness is still." Alloweth the House of Aharon now sayeth, "Thank the Lord, since He is good, since His kindness is still." Alloweth those that fear the Lord now sayeth, "Thank the Lord, since He is good, since His kindness is still."

---

237 *Pericles*, Act 4, Scene 4.
238 *Henry IV*, Part II, Act 1, Scene 2.

מִן הַמֵּצַר קָרָאתִי יָּה, עָנָנִי בַמֶּרְחַב יָה. ה' לִי, לֹא
אִירָא – מַה יַעֲשֶׂה לִי אָדָם, ה' לִי בְּעֹזְרָי וַאֲנִי
אֶרְאֶה בְשֹׂנְאָי. טוֹב לַחֲסוֹת בַּיי מִבְּטֹחַ בָּאָדָם. טוֹב
לַחֲסוֹת בַּיי מִבְּטֹחַ בִּנְדִיבִים. כָּל גּוֹיִם סְבָבוּנִי,
בְּשֵׁם ה' כִּי אֲמִילַם. סַבּוּנִי גַם סְבָבוּנִי, בְּשֵׁם ה' כִּי
אֲמִילַם. סַבּוּנִי כִדְבֹרִים, דֹּעֲכוּ כְּאֵשׁ קוֹצִים, בְּשֵׁם
ה' כִּי אֲמִילַם. דָּחֹה דְחִיתַנִי לִנְפֹּל, וַיי עֲזָרָנִי. עָזִּי
וְזִמְרָת יָה וַיְהִי לִי לִישׁוּעָה. קוֹל רִנָּה וִישׁוּעָה
בְּאָהֳלֵי צַדִּיקִים: יְמִין ה' עֹשָׂה חָיִל, יְמִין ה'
רוֹמֵמָה, יְמִין ה' עֹשָׂה חָיִל. לֹא אָמוּת כִּי אֶחְיֶה,
וַאֲסַפֵּר מַעֲשֵׂי יָה. יַסֹּר יִסְּרַנִּי יָּה, וְלַמָּוֶת לֹא נְתָנָנִי.
פִּתְחוּ לִי שַׁעֲרֵי צֶדֶק, אָבֹא בָם, אוֹדֶה יָהּ. זֶה
הַשַּׁעַר לַיי, צַדִּיקִים יָבֹאוּ בוֹ[lxiv].

lxiv *Psalms* 118:5-20.

From the strait I hast hath called, Lord. He answered me from the wide space, the Lord. The Lord is for me, I wilt not fear,[239] what wilt man doeth to me? The Lord is for me with mine helpers, and I shalt glare at those that misprise me. Tis better to taketh refuge with the Lord than to trust in man. Tis better to taketh refuge with the Lord than to trust in nobles. All the nations surrounded me, in the name of the Lord, as I wilt chop them off. They surrounded me, they eke encircled me, in the name of the Lord, as I wilt chop them off. They surrounded me like stinging bees in hottest summer's day,[240] they wast extinguished like a fire of thorns, in the name of the Lord, as I wilt chop them off. Thou hast surely pushed me to falleth, but the Lord help me. Mine boldness and song is the Lord, and he hath becometh mine salvation. The sound of joyous song and salvation is in the tents of the righteous, the right hand of the Lord acts powerfully. I wilt not die[241] but rather I wilt liveth to be thankful to thee[242] and telleth over the acts of the Lord. The Lord hath surely chastised me, but he hath not given me over to death. Ope up for me the gates of righteousness. I wilt enter them, thank the Lord. This is the gate of the Lord, the righteous wilt enter it.

---

239 *The Tempest*, Act 3, Scene 3.
240 *Titus Andronicus*, Act 5, Scene 1.
241 *Love's Labour's Lost*, Act 4, Scene 2.
242 *Twelfth Night*, Act 4, Scene 2.

אוֹדְךָ כִּי עֲנִיתָנִי וַתְּהִי לִי לִישׁוּעָה. אוֹדְךָ כִּי עֲנִיתָנִי וַתְּהִי לִי לִישׁוּעָה. אֶבֶן מָאֲסוּ הַבּוֹנִים הָיְתָה לְרֹאשׁ פִּנָּה. אֶבֶן מָאֲסוּ הַבּוֹנִים הָיְתָה לְרֹאשׁ פִּנָּה. מֵאֵת ה' הָיְתָה זֹּאת הִיא נִפְלָאת בְּעֵינֵינוּ. מֵאֵת ה' הָיְתָה זֹּאת הִיא נִפְלָאת בְּעֵינֵינוּ. זֶה הַיּוֹם עָשָׂה ה'. נָגִילָה וְנִשְׂמְחָה בוֹ. זֶה הַיּוֹם עָשָׂה ה'. נָגִילָה וְנִשְׂמְחָה בוֹ.[lxv]

אָנָּא ה', הוֹשִׁיעָה נָּא. אָנָּא ה', הוֹשִׁיעָה נָּא. אָנָּא ה', הַצְלִיחָה נָא. אָנָּא ה', הַצְלִיחָה נָא[lxvi].

בָּרוּךְ הַבָּא בְּשֵׁם ה', בֵּרַכְנוּכֶם מִבֵּית ה'. בָּרוּךְ הַבָּא בְּשֵׁם ה', בֵּרַכְנוּכֶם מִבֵּית ה'. אֵל ה' וַיָּאֶר לָנוּ. אִסְרוּ חַג בַּעֲבֹתִים עַד קַרְנוֹת הַמִּזְבֵּחַ. אֵל ה' וַיָּאֶר לָנוּ. אִסְרוּ חַג בַּעֲבֹתִים עַד קַרְנוֹת הַמִּזְבֵּחַ. אֵלִי אַתָּה וְאוֹדֶךָּ, אֱלֹהַי – אֲרוֹמְמֶךָּ. אֵלִי אַתָּה וְאוֹדֶךָּ, אֱלֹהַי – אֲרוֹמְמֶךָּ. הוֹדוּ לַיְי כִּי טוֹב, כִּי לְעוֹלָם חַסְדּוֹ. הוֹדוּ לַיְי כִּי טוֹב, כִּי לְעוֹלָם חַסְדּוֹ[lxvii].

lxv *Psalms* 118:21-24.
lxvi *Psalms* 118:25.
lxvii *Psalms* 118:26-29.

I wilt thank thee, since thee answered me and thou hast becometh mine salvation. I wilt thank thee, since thee answered me and thou hast becometh mine salvation. The stone that wast left by the builders hath becometh the main yond cornerstone.[243] The stone that wast left by the builders hath becometh the main cornerstone. From the Lord wast this, tis wondrous in our eyes. From the Lord wast this, tis wondrous in our eyes. This is the day of the Lord, alloweth us exult and rejoice upon it. This is the day of the Lord, alloweth us exult and rejoice upon it.

Please my Lord,[244] something do to save us[245] now. Please, Lord, save us now. Please, give us Lord, good success[246] now. Please, Lord, give us success now.

Blessed beest the one who cometh in the name of the Lord, we hast blessed thee from the house of the Lord. Blessed beest the one who cometh in the name of the Lord, we hast blessed thee from the house of the Lord. God is the Lord, and he hath illuminated us; tie up the festival offering with haling ropes[247] until it reacheth the corners of the altar. God is the Lord, and he hath illuminated us; tie up the festival offering with ropes until it reacheth the corners of the altar. Thee art mine Power and I wilt exalt thee. Thee art mine Power and I wilt exalt thee. Thank the Lord, since He is good, since His kindness is still. Thank the Lord, since He is good, since His kindness is still.

243 *Coriolanus*, Act 5, Scene 4.

244 *The Merchant of Venice*, Act 4, Scene 1.

245 *The Two Noble Kinsmen*, Prologue.

246 *Antony and Cleopatra*, Act 2, Scene 4.

247 *Pericles*, Act 4, Scene 1.

יְהַלְלוּךָ ה' אֱלֹהֵינוּ כָּל מַעֲשֶׂיךָ, וַחֲסִידֶיךָ צַדִּיקִים
עוֹשֵׂי רְצוֹנֶךָ, וְכָל עַמְּךָ בֵּית יִשְׂרָאֵל בְּרִנָּה יוֹדוּ
וִיבָרְכוּ, וִישַׁבְּחוּ וִיפָאֲרוּ, וִירוֹמְמוּ וְיַעֲרִיצוּ,
וְיַקְדִּישׁוּ וְיַמְלִיכוּ אֶת שִׁמְךָ, מַלְכֵּנוּ. כִּי לְךָ טוֹב
לְהוֹדוֹת וּלְשִׁמְךָ נָאֶה לְזַמֵּר, כִּי מֵעוֹלָם וְעַד עוֹלָם
אַתָּה אֵל.

All of thy work[248] shalt praise thee, Lord our God, and thy pious ones, the righteous ones who doth thy wilt; and all of thy people, the House of Israel wilt thank and bless in joyful song: and extol and glorify, and exalt and acclaim, and sanctify and coronate thy name, our commander and our King.[249] Since, thee tis valorous to thank, and to thy name tis pleasant to sing, since from at each moment and still art thee all the Power this charm doth owe.[250]

248   *Timon of Athens*, Act 1, Scene 1.
249   *The Two Gentlemen of Verona*, Act 4, Scene 1.
250   *A Midsummer Night's Dream*, Act 2, Scene 2.

שִׁירֵי שֶׁבַח וְתוֹדָה

[כּוּלָם מתחילים ללכת לחדרי השינה ולדלת הכניסה, אבל הבעל מסמן
תוך כדי שירה שיש לשתות עוד כוס אחת לפני שהלילה יסתיים. בסדר גמור.]

הוֹדוּ לַיְיָ כִּי טוֹב כִּי לְעוֹלָם חַסְדּוֹ. הוֹדוּ לֵאלֹהֵי
הָאֱלֹהִים כִּי לְעוֹלָם חַסְדּוֹ. הוֹדוּ לַאֲדֹנֵי הָאֲדֹנִים כִּי
לְעוֹלָם חַסְדּוֹ. לְעֹשֵׂה נִפְלָאוֹת גְּדֹלוֹת לְבַדּוֹ כִּי
לְעוֹלָם חַסְדּוֹ. לְעֹשֵׂה הַשָּׁמַיִם בִּתְבוּנָה כִּי לְעוֹלָם
חַסְדּוֹ. לְרוֹקַע הָאָרֶץ עַל הַמָּיִם כִּי לְעוֹלָם חַסְדּוֹ.
לְעֹשֵׂה אוֹרִים גְּדֹלִים כִּי לְעוֹלָם חַסְדּוֹ. אֶת הַשֶּׁמֶשׁ
לְמֶמְשֶׁלֶת בַּיּוֹם כִּי לְעוֹלָם חַסְדּוֹ. אֶת הַיָּרֵחַ
וְכוֹכָבִים לְמֶמְשָׁלוֹת בַּלַּיְלָה כִּי לְעוֹלָם חַסְדּוֹ. לְמַכֵּה
מִצְרַיִם בִּבְכוֹרֵיהֶם כִּי לְעוֹלָם חַסְדּוֹ. וַיּוֹצֵא יִשְׂרָאֵל
מִתּוֹכָם כִּי לְעוֹלָם חַסְדּוֹ. בְּיָד חֲזָקָה וּבִזְרוֹעַ נְטוּיָה
כִּי לְעוֹלָם חַסְדּוֹ. לְגֹזֵר יַם סוּף לִגְזָרִים כִּי לְעוֹלָם
חַסְדּוֹ. וְהֶעֱבִיר יִשְׂרָאֵל בְּתוֹכוֹ כִּי לְעוֹלָם חַסְדּוֹ.
וְנִעֵר פַּרְעֹה וְחֵילוֹ בְיַם סוּף כִּי לְעוֹלָם חַסְדּוֹ.
לְמוֹלִיךְ עַמּוֹ בַּמִּדְבָּר כִּי לְעוֹלָם חַסְדּוֹ. לְמַכֵּה
מְלָכִים גְּדֹלִים כִּי לְעוֹלָם חַסְדּוֹ. וַיַּהֲרֹג מְלָכִים
אַדִּירִים כִּי לְעוֹלָם חַסְדּוֹ. לְסִיחוֹן מֶלֶךְ הָאֱמֹרִי כִּי
לְעוֹלָם חַסְדּוֹ. וּלְעוֹג מֶלֶךְ הַבָּשָׁן כִּי לְעוֹלָם חַסְדּוֹ.

Songs of Praise and Thanks and Ever Oft Good Turns[251]

[Everyone begins heading for the bedrooms and front door, but the husband motions while singing that one more glass is to be drunk before the night is over. Fine.]

Thank the Lord, since He is good, since His kindness is still. Thank the Power of powers since His kindness is still. To the Master of masters, since His kindness is still. To the One who alone doest wondrously most wondrous deeds, since His kindness is still. To the one who madeth the Heavens with discernment, since His kindness is still. To the One who spread the earth over the waters, since His kindness is still. To the One who madeth most wondrous lights, since His kindness is still. The sun to rule in the day, since His kindness is still. The moon and the stars to rule in the night, since His kindness is still. To the One that smote Egypt through their firstborn, since His kindness is still. And He tooketh Israel out from among them, since His kindness is still. With a stout hand and an outstretched forearm, since His kindness is still. To the One who cutteth up the Reed Sea into strips, since His kindness is still. And He madeth Israel to passeth through it, since His kindness is still. And He jolted Pharaoh and his troop in the Reed Sea, since His kindness is still. To the One who hath led his people in the wilderness, since His kindness is

251 *Twelfth Night*, Act 3, Scene 3.

וְנָתַן אַרְצָם לְנַחֲלָה כִּי לְעוֹלָם חַסְדּוֹ. נַחֲלָה לְיִשְׂרָאֵל עַבְדּוֹ כִּי לְעוֹלָם חַסְדּוֹ. שֶׁבְּשִׁפְלֵנוּ זָכַר לָנוּ כִּי לְעוֹלָם חַסְדּוֹ. וַיִּפְרְקֵנוּ מִצָּרֵינוּ כִּי לְעוֹלָם חַסְדּוֹ. נֹתֵן לֶחֶם לְכָל בָּשָׂר כִּי לְעוֹלָם חַסְדּוֹ. הוֹדוּ לְאֵל הַשָּׁמַיִם כִּי לְעוֹלָם חַסְדּוֹ[lxviii].

נִשְׁמַת כָּל חַי תְּבָרֵךְ אֶת שִׁמְךָ, ה' אֱלֹהֵינוּ, וְרוּחַ כָּל בָּשָׂר תְּפָאֵר וּתְרוֹמֵם זִכְרְךָ, מַלְכֵּנוּ, תָּמִיד. מִן הָעוֹלָם וְעַד הָעוֹלָם אַתָּה אֵל, וּמִבַּלְעָדֶיךָ אֵין לָנוּ מֶלֶךְ גּוֹאֵל וּמוֹשִׁיעַ, פּוֹדֶה וּמַצִּיל וּמְפַרְנֵס וּמְרַחֵם בְּכָל עֵת צָרָה וְצוּקָה. אֵין לָנוּ מֶלֶךְ אֶלָּא אַתָּה. אֱלֹהֵי הָרִאשׁוֹנִים וְהָאַחֲרוֹנִים, אֱלוֹהַּ כָּל בְּרִיּוֹת, אֲדוֹ◌ן כָּל תּוֹלָדוֹת, הַמְהֻלָּל בְּרֹב הַתִּשְׁבָּחוֹת, הַמְנַהֵג עוֹלָמוֹ בְּחֶסֶד וּבְרִיּוֹתָיו בְּרַחֲמִים. וַיי לֹא יָנוּם וְלֹא יִישָׁן – הַמְעוֹרֵר יְשֵׁנִים וְהַמֵּקִיץ נִרְדָּמִים, וְהַמֵּשִׂיחַ אִלְּמִים וְהַמַּתִּיר אֲסוּרִים וְהַסּוֹמֵךְ נוֹפְלִים וְהַזּוֹקֵף כְּפוּפִים. לְךָ לְבַדְּךָ אֲנַחְנוּ מוֹדִים.

lxviii *Psalms* 136.

still. To the One who smote most wondrous kings, since His kindness is still. And He hath killed mighty kings, since His kindness is still. Sichon, king of the Amorite, since His kindness is still. And gentleman who holds a high estimation, king of the Bashan, since His kindness is still. And He gaveth their land as an inheritance, since His kindness is still. An inheritance for Israel, His servant, since His kindness is still. That in our lowliness, He recalled us, since His kindness is still. And He delivered us from our adversaries, since His kindness is still. He giveth bread to all flesh, since His kindness is still. Thank the Power of the heavens, since His kindness is still.

The soul of every living being shalt bless Thy Name, Lord our God; the spirit of all flesh shalt glorify and exalt Thy remembrance at each moment, our King. From the world and until the world, Thee art the Power, and other than thee there is no king,[252] dear redeemer,[253] or savior, restorer, rescuer, provider, and merciful one in every time of distress and anguish; we hast no king, besides Thee! God of the first ones and the last ones, God of all creatures, Master of all Generations, Who is praised through a multitude of praises, Who guides His world with kindness and His creatures with mercy. The Lord neither slumbers nor sleeps. He who rouses the sleepers and awakens the dozers; He who maketh the mute speaketh, and frees the captives, and supporteth the falling, and straightens the bended. We thank thee alone.

252 *Henry V*, Act 4, Scene I.
253 *Richard III*, Act 2, Scene I.

אִלּוּ פִינוּ מָלֵא שִׁירָה כַיָּם, וּלְשׁוֹנֵנוּ רִנָּה כַּהֲמוֹן
גַּלָּיו, וְשִׂפְתוֹתֵינוּ שֶׁבַח כְּמֶרְחֲבֵי רָקִיעַ, וְעֵינֵינוּ
מְאִירוֹת כַּשֶּׁמֶשׁ וְכַיָּרֵחַ, וְיָדֵינוּ פְרוּשׂוֹת כְּנִשְׁרֵי
שָׁמַיִם, וְרַגְלֵינוּ קַלּוֹת כָּאַיָּלוֹת – אֵין אֲנַחְנוּ
מַסְפִּיקִים לְהוֹדוֹת לְךָ, ה' אֱלֹהֵינוּ וֵאלֹהֵי אֲבוֹתֵינוּ,
וּלְבָרֵךְ אֶת שְׁמֶךָ עַל אַחַת מֵאֶלֶף, אַלְפֵי אֲלָפִים
וְרִבֵּי רְבָבוֹת פְּעָמִים הַטּוֹבוֹת שֶׁעָשִׂיתָ עִם אֲבוֹתֵינוּ
וְעִמָּנוּ. מִמִּצְרַיִם גְּאַלְתָּנוּ, ה' אֱלֹהֵינוּ, וּמִבֵּית
עֲבָדִים פְּדִיתָנוּ, בְּרָעָב זַנְתָּנוּ וּבְשָׂבָע כִּלְכַּלְתָּנוּ,
מֵחֶרֶב הִצַּלְתָּנוּ וּמִדֶּבֶר מִלַּטְתָּנוּ, וּמֵחֳלָיִם רָעִים
וְנֶאֱמָנִים דִּלִּיתָנוּ.

Wast our mouth as full of song as the sea, and our tongue as full of joyous song as its multitude of wild waves whist,[254] and our lips as full of praise as the breadth of the heavens, and our eyes as sparkling as the sun and the moon,[255] and our hands as outspread as the eagles of the sky and our feet as swift as deers, we still could not thank Thee sufficiently, Lord our God and God of our ancestors, and to bless thy Name for one thousandth of the thousand of thousands of thousands, and myriad myriads, of goodnesses that Thee performed for our ancestors and for us. From Egypt, Lord our God, didst Thee redeem us and from the house of slaves Thee restored us. In famine Thee nourished us, and in plenty Thee sustained us. From the sword Thee saved us, and from plague Thee spared us; and from severe and enduring diseases Thee delivered us.

---

254 *The Tempest*, Act I, Scene 2.

255 *Henry V*, Act 5, Scene 2.

עַד הֵנָּה עֲזָרוּנוּ רַחֲמֶיךָ וְלֹא עֲזָבוּנוּ חֲסָדֶיךָ, וְאַל תִּטְּשֵׁנוּ, ה' אֱלֹהֵינוּ, לָנֶצַח. עַל כֵּן אֵבָרִים שֶׁפִּלַּגְתָּ בָּנוּ וְרוּחַ וּנְשָׁמָה שֶׁנָּפַחְתָּ בְּאַפֵּינוּ וְלָשׁוֹן אֲשֶׁר שַׂמְתָּ בְּפִינוּ — הֵן הֵם יוֹדוּ וִיבָרְכוּ וִישַׁבְּחוּ וִיפָאֲרוּ וִירוֹמְמוּ וְיַעֲרִיצוּ וְיַקְדִּישׁוּ וְיַמְלִיכוּ אֶת שִׁמְךָ מַלְכֵּנוּ. כִּי כָל פֶּה לְךָ יוֹדֶה, וְכָל לָשׁוֹן לְךָ תִּשָּׁבַע, וְכָל בֶּרֶךְ לְךָ תִכְרַע, וְכָל קוֹמָה לְפָנֶיךָ תִשְׁתַּחֲוֶה, וְכָל לְבָבוֹת יִירָאוּךָ, וְכָל קֶרֶב וּכְלָיוֹת יְזַמְּרוּ לִשְׁמֶךָ. כַּדָּבָר שֶׁכָּתוּב,lxix כָּל עַצְמֹתַי תֹּאמַרְנָה, ה' מִי כָמוֹךָ מַצִּיל עָנִי מֵחָזָק מִמֶּנּוּ וְעָנִי וְאֶבְיוֹן מִגֹּזְלוֹ. מִי יִדְמֶה לָּךְ וּמִי יִשְׁוֶה לָּךְ וּמִי יַעֲרָךְ לָךְ הָאֵל הַגָּדוֹל, הַגִּבּוֹר וְהַנּוֹרָא, אֵל עֶלְיוֹן, קֹנֵה שָׁמַיִם וָאָרֶץ. נְהַלֶּלְךָ וּנְשַׁבֵּחֲךָ וּנְפָאֶרְךָ וּנְבָרֵךְ אֶת שֵׁם קָדְשֶׁךָ, כָּאָמוּר:lxx לְדָוִד, בָּרְכִי נַפְשִׁי אֶת ה' וְכָל קְרָבַי אֶת שֵׁם קָדְשׁוֹ. הָאֵל בְּתַעֲצֻמוֹת עֻזֶּךָ, הַגָּדוֹל בִּכְבוֹד שְׁמֶךָ, הַגִּבּוֹר לָנֶצַח וְהַנּוֹרָא בְּנוֹרְאוֹתֶיךָ, הַמֶּלֶךְ הַיּוֹשֵׁב עַל כִּסֵּא רָם וְנִשָּׂא. שׁוֹכֵן עַד מָרוֹם וְקָדוֹשׁ שְׁמוֹ. וְכָתוּב:lxxi רַנְּנוּ צַדִּיקִים בַּי', לַיְשָׁרִים נָאוָה תְהִלָּה. בְּפִי יְשָׁרִים תִּתְהַלָּל, וּבְדִבְרֵי צַדִּיקִים תִּתְבָּרַךְ, וּבִלְשׁוֹן חֲסִידִים תִּתְרוֹמָם, וּבְקֶרֶב קְדוֹשִׁים תִּתְקַדָּשׁ.

lxix *Psalms* 35:10.
lxx *Psalms* 103:1.
lxxi *Psalms* 33:10.

Until now Thy mercy hath helped us, and Thy kindness hath not forsaken us, and doth not abandon us, Lord our God, still. Therefore, the limbs that Thee setteth within us and the spirit and soul that Thee breathed into our nostrils, and the tongue that Thee placed in our mouth, verily, they shalt thank and bless and praise and glorify, and exalt and revere, and sanctify and coronate Thy name, our King. For every mouth shalt giveth thanks to Thee, and every tongue shalt swear allegiance to His Majesty,[256] and every knee shalt bend to Thee; and every upright one shalt prostrate himself ere Thee, all hearts shalt fear Thee, and all innermost feelings and thoughts shalt sing praises to Thy name, as the matter is writ, "All mine bones shalt sayeth, 'Lord, who is like thee? Thee save the poor man from one who is stronger than him, the poor and destitute from the one who would rob him.'" Who is similar to Thee and who is egal to Thee and who can beest compared to Thee, O most wondrous, stout and like to a silver bow[257] Power, O highest Power, Creator of the heavens and the earth. We shalt praise and extol and glorify and bless Thy holy name, as tis stated, "A Psalm to the tune of[258] David. Bless the Lord, O mine soul; and all that is within me, His holy name." The Power, in Thy powerful boldness, the most wondrous, in the glory of Thy Name, the stout One still; the King who sitteth on His high and elevated throne. He Who dwells at each moment; lofty and holy is His Name. And as tis writ, "Sing joyfully to the Lord, righteous ones, praise is quite quaint from the upright." By the mouth of the upright thee shalt beest praised. By the lips of the righteous shalt thee beest blessed. By the tongue of the devout shalt thee beest exalted. And among the holy shalt thee beest sanctified.

256 *Henry VI, Part I*, Act 5, Scene 4.

257 *A Midsummer Night's Dream*, Act 1, Scene 1.

258 *The Merry Wives of Windsor*, Act 2, Scene 1.

וּבְמַקְהֲלוֹת רִבְבוֹת עַמְּךָ בֵּית יִשְׂרָאֵל בְּרִנָּה יִתְפָּאֵר שִׁמְךָ, מַלְכֵּנוּ, בְּכָל דּוֹר וָדוֹר, שֶׁכֵּן חוֹבַת כָּל הַיְצוּרִים לְפָנֶיךָ, ה' אֱלֹהֵינוּ וֵאלֹהֵי אֲבוֹתֵינוּ, לְהוֹדוֹת לְהַלֵּל לְשַׁבֵּחַ, לְפָאֵר לְרוֹמֵם לְהַדֵּר לְבָרֵךְ, לְעַלֵּה וּלְקַלֵּס עַל כָּל דִּבְרֵי שִׁירוֹת וְתִשְׁבְּחוֹת דָּוִד בֶּן יִשַׁי עַבְדְּךָ מְשִׁיחֶךָ.

יִשְׁתַּבַּח שִׁמְךָ לָעַד מַלְכֵּנוּ, הָאֵל הַמֶּלֶךְ הַגָּדוֹל וְהַקָּדוֹשׁ בַּשָּׁמַיִם וּבָאָרֶץ, כִּי לְךָ נָאֶה, ה' אֱלֹהֵינוּ וֵאלֹהֵי אֲבוֹתֵינוּ, שִׁיר וּשְׁבָחָה, הַלֵּל וְזִמְרָה, עֹז וּמֶמְשָׁלָה, נֶצַח, גְּדֻלָּה וּגְבוּרָה, תְּהִלָּה וְתִפְאֶרֶת, קְדֻשָּׁה וּמַלְכוּת, בְּרָכוֹת וְהוֹדָאוֹת מֵעַתָּה וְעַד עוֹלָם. בָּרוּךְ אַתָּה ה', אֵל מֶלֶךְ גָּדוֹל בַּתִּשְׁבָּחוֹת, אֵל הַהוֹדָאוֹת, אֲדוֹן הַנִּפְלָאוֹת, הַבּוֹחֵר בְּשִׁירֵי זִמְרָה, מֶלֶךְ אֵל חֵי הָעוֹלָמִים.

And in assemblies[259] of the myriads of thy people, the House of Israel, in joyous song wilt thy name beest glorified, our King, in each and every generation; as tis the duty of all creatures, ere thee, Lord our God, and God of our ancestors, to thank, to praise, to extol, to glorify, to exalt, to lavish, to bless, to raiseth high and to acclaim, beyond the words of the songs and praises of David, the son of Yishai, thy servant, thy anointed deputy of heaven.[260]

May thy name beest praised still, our King, the Power, the most wondrous and holy King, in the heavens and in the earth. Since for Thee tis, by my troth, most pleasant,[261] O Lord our God and God of our ancestors, song and lauding, praise and hymn, boldness and dominion, triumph, greatness and strength, psalm and splendor, holiness and kingship, blessings and thanksgivings, from now and still. Blessed art Thee Lord, Power, King exalted through laudings, Power of thanksgivings, Master of Wonders, who chooseth the songs of hymn,-King, Power of the life of the worlds.

259 *The Comedy of Errors*, Act 5, Scene 1.
260 *King John*, Act 3, Scene 1.
261 *Love's Labour's Lost*, Act 4, Scene 1.

כּוֹס רְבִיעִי

בָּרוּךְ אַתָּה ה', אֱלֹהֵינוּ מֶלֶךְ הָעוֹלָם בּוֹרֵא פְּרִי הַגָּפֶן.

וְשׁוֹתֶה בַּהֲסִבַּת שְׂמֹאל.

בָּרוּךְ אַתָּה ה' אֱלֹהֵינוּ מֶלֶךְ הָעוֹלָם, עַל הַגֶּפֶן וְעַל פְּרִי הַגֶּפֶן, עַל תְּנוּבַת הַשָּׂדֶה וְעַל אֶרֶץ חֶמְדָּה טוֹבָה וּרְחָבָה שֶׁרָצִיתָ וְהִנְחַלְתָּ לַאֲבוֹתֵינוּ לֶאֱכוֹל מִפִּרְיָהּ וְלִשְׂבֹּעַ מִטּוּבָהּ. רַחֶם נָא ה' אֱלֹהֵינוּ עַל יִשְׂרָאֵל עַמֶּךָ וְעַל יְרוּשָׁלַיִם עִירֶךָ וְעַל צִיּוֹן מִשְׁכַּן כְּבוֹדֶךָ וְעַל מִזְבְּחֶךָ וְעַל הֵיכָלֶךָ וּבְנֵה יְרוּשָׁלַיִם עִיר הַקֹּדֶשׁ בִּמְהֵרָה בְּיָמֵינוּ וְהַעֲלֵנוּ לְתוֹכָהּ וְשַׂמְּחֵנוּ בְּבִנְיָנָהּ וְנֹאכַל מִפִּרְיָהּ וְנִשְׂבַּע מִטּוּבָהּ וּנְבָרֶכְךָ עָלֶיהָ בִּקְדֻשָׁה וּבְטָהֳרָה [בשבת: וּרְצֵה וְהַחֲלִיצֵנוּ בְּיוֹם הַשַּׁבָּת הַזֶּה] וְשַׂמְּחֵנוּ בְּיוֹם חַג הַמַּצּוֹת הַזֶּה, כִּי אַתָּה ה' טוֹב וּמֵטִיב לַכֹּל, וְנוֹדֶה לְּךָ עַל הָאָרֶץ וְעַל פְּרִי הַגָּפֶן.

בָּרוּךְ אַתָּה ה', עַל הָאָרֶץ וְעַל פְּרִי הַגָּפֶן.

150

Fourth Hogshead of Wine[262]

Blessed art Thee, Lord our God, King of the universe, who maketh the fruit of the vine.

We drinketh while reclining to the left.

Blessed art Thee, Lord our God, King of the universe, for the vine and for the fruit of the vine; and for the bounty of the field; and for a desirable, good and broad land, which Thee wanted to giveth to our fathers, to consume from its fruit and to beest satiated from its goodness. Please hast mercy, Lord our God upon Israel Thy people; and upon Jerusalem, Thy city, and upon Zion, the lodging of Thy glory, and upon Thy altar; and upon Thy sanctuary, and buildeth Jerusalem Thy holy city apace in our days, and bringeth us up into it and gladden us in its building; and we shalt consume from its fruit, and beest satiated from its goodness, and bless Thee in holiness and purity. [On Shabbat: And may thee beest pleased to embolden us on this Shabbat day] and gladden us on this day of the Festival of Unleavened Breads. Since Thee, Lord, art good and doeth good to all, we thank Thee for the land and for the fruit of the vine.

Blessed art Thee, Lord, for the land and for the fruit of the vine.

---

262 *The Tempest*, Act 4, Scene 1.

נִרְצָה

To Be Accepted of and Stood Upon[263]

—

ACT V

263 *King Edward III*, Act 4, Scene 3.

חֲסַל סִדּוּר פֶּסַח

חֲסַל סִדּוּר פֶּסַח כְּהִלְכָתוֹ, כְּכָל מִשְׁפָּטוֹ וְחֻקָּתוֹ.
כַּאֲשֶׁר זָכִינוּ לְסַדֵּר אוֹתוֹ כֵּן נִזְכֶּה לַעֲשׂוֹתוֹ. זָךְ
שׁוֹכֵן מְעוֹנָה, קוֹמֵם קְהַל עֲדַת מִי מָנָה. בְּקָרוֹב נַהֵל
נִטְעֵי כַנָּה פְּדוּיִם לְצִיּוֹן בְּרִנָּה.

Completed Is the Order of Passover

Completed is the order of Passover accountant to the law,[264] according to all its judgement and statute. Just as we hast merited to arrange it, so too, may we merit to doeth. Pure One who dwells in the habitation, raiseth up the congregation of the community, which whom can count. Bringeth close, leadeth the plantings of the tender sapling,[265] redeemed, to Zion in joy.

---

264   *Measure for Measure*, Act 2, Scene 4.
265   *Titus Andronicus*, Act 3, Scene 2.

לְשָׁנָה הַבָּאָה

לְשָׁנָה הַבָּאָה בִּירוּשָׁלַיִם הַבְּנוּיָה!

[האורחים הולכים אל הדלת, והבעל מלווה אותם. זה כבר מאוחר מדי
עבור המחותנים להיות ערים, אז הם פורשים. כשהבעל מתחיל את השיר הבא,
הוא נושא את הקטן למיטה. שני הבנים הבאים זוממים הולכים למיטה בעצמם.
נשארו רק האשה והבן החכם.]

Next Year[266]

Next year, alloweth us beest in the hath built Jerusalem!

[The guests head for the door, and the husband sees them off. It's way too late for the in-laws to be up, so they retire. As the husband begins the next song, he carries the youngest off to bed. The next two sons zombie-walk to bed themselves. Only the wife and the Wise Son are left.]

---

266 *All's Well That Ends Well*, Act 2, Scene 1.

וַיְהִי בַּחֲצִי הַלַּיְלָה

בליל רִאשׁוֹן אומרים:

וּבְכֵן וַיְהִי בַּחֲצִי הַלַּיְלָה.

אָז רוֹב נִסִּים הִפְלֵאתָ בַּלַּיְלָה, בְּרֹאשׁ אַשְׁמוֹרֶת זֶה
הַלַּיְלָה.

גֵּר צֶדֶק נִצַּחְתּוֹ כְּנֶחֱלַק לוֹ לַיְלָה,[lxxii] וַיְהִי בַּחֲצִי
הַלַּיְלָה.

דַּנְתָּ מֶלֶךְ גְּרָר בַּחֲלוֹם הַלַּיְלָה, הִפְחַדְתָּ אֲרַמִּי
בְּאֶמֶשׁ לַיְלָה.

וַיָּשַׂר יִשְׂרָאֵל לְמַלְאָךְ וַיּוּכַל לוֹ לַיְלָה,[lxxiii] וַיְהִי
בַּחֲצִי הַלַּיְלָה.

זֶרַע בְּכוֹרֵי פַתְרוֹס[lxxiv] מָחַצְתָּ בַּחֲצִי הַלַּיְלָה, חֵילָם
לֹא מָצְאוּ בְּקוּמָם בַּלַּיְלָה, טִיסַת נְגִיד חֲרֹשֶׁת סִלִּיתָ
בְּכוֹכְבֵי לַיְלָה,[lxxv] וַיְהִי בַּחֲצִי הַלַּיְלָה.

[lxxii] *Genesis* 14:15.
[lxxiii] *Genesis* 32:25-30.
[lxxiv] *Ezekiel* 30:14.
[lxxv] *Judges* 5:20.

And It Happened,
As They Say Spirits Do,
at Midnight[267]

On the first night we sayeth:

And so, twas upon the heavy middle of the night.[268]

Then, most of the miracles didst Thee wondrously doeth at night, at the first of the gazes this night.

A righteous convert didst Thee maketh victorious at which hour twas divided for Him at night, and twas in the dead waste and the middle of the night.[269]

Thee judged the king of Gerrar in a dream of the night, Thee frightened an Aramean in the dark of the night.

And Yisrael dominated an angel and wast able to withstand Him at night, and twas in the middle of the night.

Thee crushed the firstborn of Patros in the middle of the night, their wealth they didst not findeth at which hour they got up at night. The attack of the vaward Charoshet didst Thee sweep hence by the stars of the night, and twas in the middle of the night.

---

267 *Henry VIII*, Act 5, Scene 1.
268 *Measure for Measure*, Act 4, Scene 1.
269 *Hamlet*, Act 1, Scene 2.

יָעַץ מְחָרֵף לְנוֹפֵף אִוּוּי, הוֹבַשְׁתָּ פְּגָרָיו בַּלַּיְלָה, [lxxvi]
כָּרַע בֵּל וּמַצָּבוֹ בְּאִישׁוֹן לַיְלָה, [lxxvii] לְאִישׁ חֲמוּדוֹת
נִגְלָה רָז חֲזוֹת לַיְלָה, וַיְהִי בַּחֲצִי הַלַּיְלָה.

מִשְׁתַּכֵּר בִּכְלֵי קֹדֶשׁ נֶהֱרַג בּוֹ בַּלַּיְלָה, [lxxviii] נוֹשַׁע
מִבּוֹר אֲרָיוֹת פּוֹתֵר בִּעֲתוּתֵי לַיְלָה, שִׂנְאָה נָטַר אֲגָגִי
וְכָתַב סְפָרִים בַּלַּיְלָה, וַיְהִי בַּחֲצִי הַלַּיְלָה.

עוֹרַרְתָּ נִצְחֲךָ עָלָיו בְּנֶדֶד שְׁנַת לַיְלָה. פּוּרָה תִדְרוֹךְ
לְשׁוֹמֵר מַה מִלַּיְלָה, [lxxix] צָרַח כַּשׁוֹמֵר וְשָׂח אָתָא
בֹקֶר וְגַם לַיְלָה, וַיְהִי בַּחֲצִי הַלַּיְלָה.

קָרֵב יוֹם אֲשֶׁר הוּא לֹא יוֹם וְלֹא לַיְלָה, רָם הוֹדַע
כִּי לְךָ הַיּוֹם אַף לְךָ הַלַּיְלָה, [lxxx] שׁוֹמְרִים הַפְקֵד
לְעִירְךָ כָּל הַיּוֹם וְכָל הַלַּיְלָה, תָּאִיר כְּאוֹר יוֹם
חֶשְׁכַת לַיְלָה, וַיְהִי בַּחֲצִי הַלַּיְלָה.

[lxxvi] *II Kings*, 19:35.
[lxxvii] Daniel 2.
[lxxviii] *Daniel* 5:30.
[lxxix] *Isaiah* 21:11.
[lxxx] Zechariah 14:7.

The blasphemer counseled to waft off the desired ones, thee madeth him wear his corpses on his head at night, Bel and his pedestal wast bended in the pitch of night, to the man of delight wast revealed the secret visions at night, and twas in the middle of the night.

The one who got drunk from the holy vessels wast killed on that night, the one saved from the pit of lions interpreted the scary visions of the night, hatred wast preserved by the Agagite and he wroteth books at night, and twas in the middle of the night.

Thee aroused and roared away thy victory[270] upon him by disturbing the sleep of night, Thee wilt stomp the wine press for the one who guards from anything at night, he yelled like a guard and spake, "the morning hath cometh and eke the night," and twas in the middle of the night.

Bringeth close the day which is not day and not night, High One, maketh known that Thine is the day and eke Thine is the night, guards appoint for Thy city all the day and all the night, illuminate like the light of the day, the darkness of the night, and twas in the middle of the night.

270 *Coriolanus*, Act 5, Scene 4.

זֶבַח פֶּסַח

וּבְכֵן וַאֲמַרְתֶּם זֶבַח פֶּסַח lxxxi.

אֹמֶץ גְּבוּרוֹתֶיךָ הִפְלֵאתָ בַּפֶּסַח, בְּרֹאשׁ כָּל מוֹעֲדוֹת נִשֵּׂאתָ פֶּסַח. גִּלִּיתָ לְאֶזְרָחִי חֲצוֹת לֵיל פֶּסַח, וַאֲמַרְתֶּם זֶבַח פֶּסַח.

דְּלָתָיו דָּפַקְתָּ כְּחֹם הַיּוֹם בַּפֶּסַח, lxxxii הִסְעִיד נוֹצְצִים עֻגוֹת מַצּוֹת בַּפֶּסַח, וְאֶל הַבָּקָר רָץ זֵכֶר לְשׁוֹר עֶרֶךְ פֶּסַח, וַאֲמַרְתֶּם זֶבַח פֶּסַח.

זוֹעֲמוּ סְדוֹמִים וְלוֹהֲטוּ בָּאֵשׁ בַּפֶּסַח, חֻלַּץ לוֹט מֵהֶם וּמַצּוֹת אָפָה בְּקֵץ פֶּסַח, טִאטֵאתָ אַדְמַת מוֹף וְנוֹף בְּעָבְרְךָ בַּפֶּסַח. וַאֲמַרְתֶּם זֶבַח פֶּסַח.

lxxxii *Genesis* 18:1.

The Passover Sacrifice

On the second night, outside of Israel:

And so "And thee shalt sayeth, 'it is the Passover sacrifice.'"

The boldness of thy stout deeds didst Thee wondrously showeth at Passover, at the head of all the holidays didst thee raiseth Passover. Thee revealed to the Ezrachite, chimes at midnight[271] of the night of Passover. "And thee shalt sayeth, 'it is the Passover sacrifice.'"

Upon his doors didst Thee knock at the heat of day[272] on Passover, he sustained shining ones with dried cakes[273] of unleavened bread on Passover, and to the cattle he ranneth, in commemoration of the bull that wast setteth up for Passover. "And thee shalt sayeth, 'it is the Passover sacrifice.'"

The Sodomites caused Him indignation and He setteth them on fire on Passover, Lot wast rescued from them and unleavened bread didst he bake at the end of Passover, He swept the land of Mof and Nof on Passover. "And thee shalt sayeth, 'it is the Passover sacrifice.'"

---

271 *Henry IV<*,Part II, Act 3, Scene 2.

272 *Ibid*, Act 4, Scene 5.

273 *Ibid*, Act 2, Scene 4.

יָה רֹאשׁ כָּל הוֹן מָחַצְתָּ בְּלֵיל שָׁמוּר פֶּסַח, כַּבִּיר,
עַל בֵּן בְּכוֹר פָּסַחְתָּ בְּדַם פֶּסַח, לְבִלְתִּי תֵּת מַשְׁחִית
לָבֹא בִּפְתָחַי בַּפֶּסַח, וַאֲמַרְתֶּם זֶבַח פֶּסַח.

מִסְגֶּרֶת סֻגָּרָה בְּעִתּוֹתֵי פֶּסַח, נִשְׁמְדָה מִדְיָן בִּצְלִיל
שְׂעוֹרֵי עֹמֶר פֶּסַח,lxxxiii שֹׁרָפוּ מִשְׁמַנֵּי פוּל וְלוּד
בִּיקַד יְקוֹד פֶּסַח, וַאֲמַרְתֶּם זֶבַח פֶּסַח.

עוֹד הַיּוֹם בְּנֹבlxxxiv לַעֲמוֹד עַד גָּעָה עוֹנַת פֶּסַח, פַּס
יַד כָּתְבָהlxxxv לְקַעֲקֵעַ צוּל בַּפֶּסַח, צָפֹה הַצָּפִית עָרוֹךְ
הַשֻּׁלְחָן בַּפֶּסַחlxxxvi, וַאֲמַרְתֶּם זֶבַח פֶּסַח.

קָהָל כִּנְּסָה הֲדַסָּה לְשַׁלֵּשׁ צוֹם בַּפֶּסַח, רֹאשׁ מִבֵּית
רָשָׁע מָחַצְתָּ בְּעֵץ חֲמִשִּׁים בַּפֶּסַח, שְׁתֵּי אֵלֶּהlxxxvii
רֶגַע תָּבִיא לְעוּצִית בַּפֶּסַח, תָּעֹז יָדְךָ תָּרוּם יְמִינְךָ
כְּלֵיל הִתְקַדֶּשׁ חַג פֶּסַח, וַאֲמַרְתֶּם זֶבַח פֶּסַח.

lxxxiii Judges 7.
lxxxiv Isaiah 10:32.
lxxxv Daniel 5:5.
lxxxvi Psalms 21:5.
lxxxvii Isaiah 47:9.

The head of every firstborn didst Thee crush on the guarded night of Passover, Powerful One, over the firstborn son didst Thee passeth over with the blood on Passover, so as to not alloweth the destroyer cometh into mine gates on Passover. "And thee shalt sayeth, 'it is the Passover sacrifice.'"

The enclosed one wast enclosed in the season of Passover, Midian wast destroyed with a moiety of the omer-barley on Passover, from the fat of Pul and Lud wast burnt in pyres on Passover. "And thee shalt sayeth, 'it is the Passover sacrifice.'"

Still the present day to standeth in Nov, until he cried at the time of Passover, a palm of the hand[274] wroteth to rip up the deep one on Passover, setteth up the gaze, setteth the table[275]]on Passover. "And thee shalt sayeth, 'it is the Passover sacrifice'"

The congregation didst Hadassah bringeth in to triple a fast on Passover, the head of the house of evil didst Thee crush on a tree of fifty on Passover, these two wilt thee bringeth in an instant to the Utsi on Passover, embolden thy hand, raiseth thy right hand, as on the night thee wast sanctified on the festival of Passover. "And thee shalt sayeth, 'it is the Passover sacrifice.'"

274 *The Comedy of Errors*, Act 3, Scene 2.
275 *Hamlet*, Act 5, Scene 1.

כִּי לוֹ נָאֶה

כִּי לוֹ נָאֶה, כִּי לוֹ יָאֶה.

אַדִּיר בִּמְלוּכָה, בָּחוּר כַּהֲלָכָה, גְּדוּדָיו יֹאמְרוּ לוֹ:
לְךָ וּלְךָ, לְךָ כִּי לְךָ, לְךָ אַף לְךָ, לְךָ ה' הַמַּמְלָכָה,
כִּי לוֹ נָאֶה, כִּי לוֹ יָאֶה.

דָּגוּל בִּמְלוּכָה, הָדוּר כַּהֲלָכָה, וָתִיקָיו יֹאמְרוּ לוֹ:
לְךָ וּלְךָ, לְךָ כִּי לְךָ, לְךָ אַף לְךָ, לְךָ ה' הַמַּמְלָכָה,
כִּי לוֹ נָאֶה, כִּי לוֹ יָאֶה.

זַכַּאי בִּמְלוּכָה, חָסִין כַּהֲלָכָה טַפְסְרָיו יֹאמְרוּ לוֹ:
לְךָ וּלְךָ, לְךָ כִּי לְךָ, לְךָ אַף לְךָ, לְךָ ה' הַמַּמְלָכָה,
כִּי לוֹ נָאֶה, כִּי לוֹ יָאֶה.

יָחִיד בִּמְלוּכָה, כַּבִּיר כַּהֲלָכָה לִמּוּדָיו יֹאמְרוּ לוֹ: לְךָ
וּלְךָ, לְךָ כִּי לְךָ, לְךָ אַף לְךָ, לְךָ ה' הַמַּמְלָכָה, כִּי לוֹ
נָאֶה, כִּי לוֹ יָאֶה.

Since for Him Tis Pleasant

Since for Him tis pleasant, for Him tis suited.

Mighty in rulership, properly chosen, his troops shalt sayeth to Him, "Thine and Thine, Thine since tis Thine, Thine and coequal Thine, Thine, Lord is the kingdom, since for Him tis pleasant, for Him tis suited."

Noted in rulership, properly splendid, His distinguished ones wilt sayeth to Him, "Thine and Thine, Thine since tis Thine, Thine and coequal Thine, Thine, Lord is the kingdom, since for Him tis pleasant, for Him tis suited."

Meritorious in rulership, properly robust, His scribes, bards, poets[276] wilt sayeth to him, "Thine and Thine, Thine since tis Thine, Thine and coequal Thine, Thine, Lord is the kingdom, since for Him tis pleasant, for Him tis suited."

Unique in rulership, properly powerful, His fair and wise ones do[277] sayeth to Him, "Thine and Thine, Thine since tis Thine, Thine and coequal Thine, Thine, Lord is the kingdom, since for Him tis pleasant, for Him tis suited."

---

276 *Antony and Cleopatra*, Act 3, Scene 2.
277 *Othello*, Act 2, Scene 1.

מוֹשֵׁל בִּמְלוּכָה, נוֹרָא כַּהֲלָכָה סְבִיבָיו יֹאמְרוּ לוֹ:
לְךָ וּלְךָ, לְךָ כִּי לְךָ, לְךָ אַף לְךָ, לְךָ ה' הַמַּמְלָכָה,
כִּי לוֹ נָאֶה, כִּי לוֹ יָאֶה.

עָנָיו בִּמְלוּכָה, פּוֹדֶה כַּהֲלָכָה, צַדִּיקָיו יֹאמְרוּ לוֹ:
לְךָ וּלְךָ, לְךָ כִּי לְךָ, לְךָ אַף לְךָ, לְךָ ה' הַמַּמְלָכָה,
כִּי לוֹ נָאֶה, כִּי לוֹ יָאֶה.

קָדוֹשׁ בִּמְלוּכָה, רַחוּם כַּהֲלָכָה שִׁנְאַנָּיו יֹאמְרוּ לוֹ:
לְךָ וּלְךָ, לְךָ כִּי לְךָ, לְךָ אַף לְךָ, לְךָ ה' הַמַּמְלָכָה,
כִּי לוֹ נָאֶה, כִּי לוֹ יָאֶה.

תַּקִּיף בִּמְלוּכָה, תּוֹמֵךְ כַּהֲלָכָה תְּמִימָיו יֹאמְרוּ לוֹ:
לְךָ וּלְךָ, לְךָ כִּי לְךָ, לְךָ אַף לְךָ, לְךָ ה' הַמַּמְלָכָה,
כִּי לוֹ נָאֶה, כִּי לוֹ יָאֶה.

Reigning in rulership, properly like to a silver bow,[278] those around Him sayeth to Him, "Thine and Thine, Thine since tis Thine, Thine and coequal Thine, Thine, Lord is the kingdom, since for Him tis pleasant, for Him tis suited."

Humble in rulership, properly restoring, His righteous ones sayeth to Him, "Thine and Thine, Thine since tis Thine, Thine and coequal Thine, Thine, Lord is the kingdom, since for Him tis pleasant, for Him tis suited."

Holy in rulership, properly merciful, His angels sayeth to Him, "Thine and Thine, Thine since tis Thine, Thine and coequal Thine, Thine, Lord is the kingdom, since for Him tis pleasant, for Him tis suited."

Dynamic in rulership, properly supportive, His sweet and innocent[279] ones sayeth to Him, "Thine and Thine, Thine since tis Thine, Thine and coequal Thine, Thine, Lord is the kingdom, since for Him tis pleasant, for Him tis suited."

---

278 *A Midsummer Night's Dream*, Act I, Scene I.
279 *Much Ado About Nothing*, Act 5, Scene I.

אַדִּיר הוּא

אַדִּיר הוּא יִבְנֶה בֵּיתוֹ בְּקָרוֹב. בִּמְהֵרָה, בִּמְהֵרָה,
בְּיָמֵינוּ בְּקָרוֹב. אֵל בְּנֵה, אֵל בְּנֵה, בְּנֵה בֵּיתְךָ בְּקָרוֹב.

בָּחוּר הוּא, גָּדוֹל הוּא, דָּגוּל הוּא יִבְנֶה בֵּיתוֹ בְּקָרוֹב.
בִּמְהֵרָה, בִּמְהֵרָה, בְּיָמֵינוּ בְּקָרוֹב. אֵל בְּנֵה, אֵל בְּנֵה,
בְּנֵה בֵּיתְךָ בְּקָרוֹב.

הָדוּר הוּא, וָתִיק הוּא, זַכַּאי הוּא יִבְנֶה בֵּיתוֹ בְּקָרוֹב.
בִּמְהֵרָה, בִּמְהֵרָה, בְּיָמֵינוּ בְּקָרוֹב. אֵל בְּנֵה, אֵל בְּנֵה,
בְּנֵה בֵּיתְךָ בְּקָרוֹב.

חָסִיד הוּא, טָהוֹר הוּא, יָחִיד הוּא יִבְנֶה בֵּיתוֹ בְּקָרוֹב.
בִּמְהֵרָה, בִּמְהֵרָה, בְּיָמֵינוּ בְּקָרוֹב. אֵל בְּנֵה, אֵל בְּנֵה,
בְּנֵה בֵּיתְךָ בְּקָרוֹב.

כַּבִּיר הוּא, לָמוּד הוּא, מֶלֶךְ הוּא יִבְנֶה בֵּיתוֹ בְּקָרוֹב.
בִּמְהֵרָה, בִּמְהֵרָה, בְּיָמֵינוּ בְּקָרוֹב. אֵל בְּנֵה, אֵל בְּנֵה,
בְּנֵה בֵּיתְךָ בְּקָרוֹב.

נוֹרָא הוּא, סַגִּיב הוּא, עִזּוּז הוּא יִבְנֶה בֵּיתוֹ בְּקָרוֹב.
בִּמְהֵרָה, בִּמְהֵרָה, בְּיָמֵינוּ בְּקָרוֹב. אֵל בְּנֵה, אֵל בְּנֵה,
בְּנֵה בֵּיתְךָ בְּקָרוֹב.

Mighty Is He

A Mighty Power[280] is He, may He buildeth His house soon. Apace, apace, in our days, soon. God buildeh, buildeth thy house soon.

Pious is He, pure is He, alone is He. Apace, apace, in our days, soon. God buildeth, God buildeth, buildeth thy house soon.

Powerful is He, wise is He, A king is He. Apace, apace, in our days, soon. God buildeth, God buildeth, buildeth thy house soon.

Like a silver bow is He, exalted is He, heroic is He. Apace, apace, in our days, soon. God buildeth, God buildeth, buildeth thy house soon.

A restorer is He, righteous is He, holy is He. Apace, apace, in our days, soon. God buildeth, God buildeth, buildeth thy house soon.

Merciful is He, the God Omnipotent[281] is He, dynamic is He. Apace, apace, in our days, soon. God buildeth, God buildeth, buildeth thy house soon.

Like a silver bow is He, exalted is He, heroic is He. Apace, apace, in our days, soon. God buildeth, God buildeth, buildeth thy house soon.

---

280 *As You Like It*, Act 5, Scene 4.
281 *Richard II*, Act 3, Scene 3.

פוֹדֶה הוּא, צַדִּיק הוּא, קָדוֹשׁ הוּא יִבְנֶה בֵּיתוֹ בְּקָרוֹב. בִּמְהֵרָה, בִּמְהֵרָה, בְּיָמֵינוּ בְּקָרוֹב. אֵל בְּנֵה, אֵל בְּנֵה, בְּנֵה בֵיתְךָ בְּקָרוֹב.

רַחוּם הוּא, שַׁדַּי הוּא, תַּקִּיף הוּא יִבְנֶה בֵּיתוֹ בְּקָרוֹב. בִּמְהֵרָה, בִּמְהֵרָה, בְּיָמֵינוּ בְּקָרוֹב. אֵל בְּנֵה, אֵל בְּנֵה, בְּנֵה בֵיתְךָ בְּקָרוֹב.

A restorer is He, righteous is He, holy is He. Apace, apace, in our days, soon. God buildeth, God buildeth, buildeth thy house soon.

Merciful is He, the God Omnipotent[282] is He, dynamic is He. Apace, apace, in our days, soon. God buildeth, God buildeth, buildeth thy house soon.

282 Richard II, Act 3, Scene 3.

סְפִירַת הָעֹמֶר

ספירת העמר בחוץ לארץ, בליל שני של פסח:

בָּרוּךְ אַתָּה ה', אֱלֹהֵינוּ מֶלֶךְ הָעוֹלָם, אֲשֶׁר קִדְּשָׁנוּ בְּמִצְוֹתָיו וְצִוָּנוּ עַל סְפִירַת הָעֹמֶר. הַיּוֹם יוֹם אֶחָד בָּעֹמֶר.

[הבן החכם נשאר ער כדי לוודא שכולם מבצעים את ההקפדה הזו כמו שצריך. חבל שנותרו רק שלושה אנשים. זה סוף הדרך מבחינתו. בחייך, קדימה, השעה 1:47 לפנות בוקר. רק הבעל והאישה עכשיו. האישה אוהבת את אחד מי יודע, והיא אוהבת לשיר אותו בשפה זרה מעניינת.]

The Counting of the Omer

The counting of the omer outside of Israel on the second night[283] of Pesach:

Blessed art Thee, Lord our God, King of the universe, who hath sanctified us with His commandments and hath commanded us on the counting of the omer. Whence this present day[284] is fresh as the first day[285] of the omer.

> *[The Wise Son remained up to make sure everyone carries out this stringency properly. Too bad there are only three people left. This is the end of the road for him. I mean, c'mon, It's 1:47 in the morning. Just the husband and wife now. The wife likes Who Knoweth One, and she likes to sing it in an interesting foreign language.]*

---

283 *Cymbeline*, Act 2, Scene 4.

284 *Richard III*, Act 1, Scene 1.

285 *The Tempest*, Act 2, Scene 1.

אֶחָד מִי יוֹדֵעַ?

אֶחָד מִי יוֹדֵעַ? אֶחָד אֲנִי יוֹדֵעַ: אֶחָד אֱלֹהֵינוּ שֶׁבַּשָׁמַיִם וּבָאָרֶץ.

שְׁנַיִם מִי יוֹדֵעַ? שְׁנַיִם אֲנִי יוֹדֵעַ: שְׁנֵי לֻחוֹת הַבְּרִית. אֶחָד אֱלֹהֵינוּ שֶׁבַּשָׁמַיִם וּבָאָרֶץ.

שְׁלֹשָׁה מִי יוֹדֵעַ? שְׁלֹשָׁה אֲנִי יוֹדֵעַ: שְׁלֹשָׁה אָבוֹת, שְׁנֵי לֻחוֹת הַבְּרִית, אֶחָד אֱלֹהֵינוּ שֶׁבַּשָׁמַיִם וּבָאָרֶץ.

אַרְבַּע מִי יוֹדֵעַ? אַרְבַּע אֲנִי יוֹדֵעַ: אַרְבַּע אִמָּהוֹת, שְׁלֹשָׁה אָבוֹת, שְׁנֵי לֻחוֹת הַבְּרִית, אֶחָד אֱלֹהֵינוּ שֶׁבַּשָׁמַיִם וּבָאָרֶץ.

חֲמִשָּׁה מִי יוֹדֵעַ? חֲמִשָּׁה אֲנִי יוֹדֵעַ: חֲמִשָּׁה חוּמְשֵׁי תוֹרָה, אַרְבַּע אִמָּהוֹת, שְׁלֹשָׁה אָבוֹת, שְׁנֵי לֻחוֹת הַבְּרִית, אֶחָד אֱלֹהֵינוּ שֶׁבַּשָׁמַיִם וּבָאָרֶץ.

שִׁשָּׁה מִי יוֹדֵעַ? שִׁשָּׁה אֲנִי יוֹדֵעַ: שִׁשָּׁה סִדְרֵי מִשְׁנָה, חֲמִשָּׁה חוּמְשֵׁי תוֹרָה, אַרְבַּע אִמָּהוֹת, שְׁלֹשָׁה אָבוֹת, שְׁנֵי לֻחוֹת הַבְּרִית, אֶחָד אֱלֹהֵינוּ שֶׁבַּשָׁמַיִם וּבָאָרֶץ.

Alas, Who Knoweth[286] One?

Who knoweth of the one?[287] I knoweth one: One is our God in the heavens and the earth.

Who knoweth but for two?[288] I knoweth two: two art the tablets of the covenant, One is our God in the heavens and the earth.

Who knoweth the company of three?[289] I knoweth three: three art the fathers, two art the tablets of the covenant, One is our God in the heavens and the earth.

Who knoweth ay, four?[290] I knoweth four: four art the mothers, three art the fathers, two art the tablets of the covenant, One is our God in the heavens and the earth.

Who knoweth of the fives?[291] I knoweth five: five art the books of the Torah, four art the mothers, three art the fathers, two art the tablets of the covenant, One is our God in the heavens and the earth.

Who knoweth what's the sixth?[292] I knoweth six: six art the orders of the Mishnah, five art the books of the Torah, four art the mothers, three art the fathers, two art the tablets of the covenant, One is our God in the heavens and the earth.

---

286 *Othello*, Act 5, Scene 2.
287 *The Winter's Tale*, Act 5, Scene 2.
288 *All's Well That Ends Well*, Act 2, Scene 4.
289 *The Two Gentlemen of Verona*, Act 4, Scene 4.
290 *Henry IV*, Part I, Act 2, Scene 4.
291 *The Taming of the Shrew*, Act 3, Scene 2.
292 *Pericles*, Act 2, Scene 2.

שִׁבְעָה מִי יוֹדֵעַ? שִׁבְעָה אֲנִי יוֹדֵעַ: שִׁבְעָה יְמֵי שַׁבַּתָּא, שִׁשָּׁה סִדְרֵי מִשְׁנָה, חֲמִשָּׁה חוּמְשֵׁי תוֹרָה, אַרְבַּע אִמָּהוֹת, שְׁלֹשָׁה אָבוֹת, שְׁנֵי לֻחוֹת הַבְּרִית, אֶחָד אֱלֹהֵינוּ שֶׁבַּשָּׁמַיִם וּבָאָרֶץ.

שְׁמוֹנָה מִי יוֹדֵעַ? שְׁמוֹנָה אֲנִי יוֹדֵעַ: שְׁמוֹנָה יְמֵי מִילָה, שִׁבְעָה יְמֵי שַׁבַּתָּא, שִׁשָּׁה סִדְרֵי מִשְׁנָה, חֲמִשָּׁה חוּמְשֵׁי תוֹרָה, אַרְבַּע אִמָּהוֹת, שְׁלֹשָׁה אָבוֹת, שְׁנֵי לֻחוֹת הַבְּרִית, אֶחָד אֱלֹהֵינוּ שֶׁבַּשָּׁמַיִם וּבָאָרֶץ.

תִּשְׁעָה מִי יוֹדֵעַ? תִּשְׁעָה אֲנִי יוֹדֵעַ: תִּשְׁעָה יַרְחֵי לֵדָה, שְׁמוֹנָה יְמֵי מִילָה, שִׁבְעָה יְמֵי שַׁבַּתָּא, שִׁשָּׁה סִדְרֵי מִשְׁנָה, חֲמִשָּׁה חוּמְשֵׁי תוֹרָה, אַרְבַּע אִמָּהוֹת, שְׁלֹשָׁה אָבוֹת, שְׁנֵי לֻחוֹת הַבְּרִית, אֶחָד אֱלֹהֵינוּ שֶׁבַּשָּׁמַיִם וּבָאָרֶץ.

עֲשָׂרָה מִי יוֹדֵעַ? עֲשָׂרָה אֲנִי יוֹדֵעַ: עֲשָׂרָה דִבְּרַיָּא, תִּשְׁעָה יַרְחֵי לֵדָה, שְׁמוֹנָה יְמֵי מִילָה, שִׁבְעָה יְמֵי שַׁבַּתָּא, שִׁשָּׁה סִדְרֵי מִשְׁנָה, חֲמִשָּׁה חוּמְשֵׁי תוֹרָה, אַרְבַּע אִמָּהוֹת, שְׁלֹשָׁה אָבוֹת, שְׁנֵי לֻחוֹת הַבְּרִית, אֶחָד אֱלֹהֵינוּ שֶׁבַּשָּׁמַיִם וּבָאָרֶץ.

Who knoweth a seventh?[293] I knoweth seven: seven art the days of the week, six art the orders of the Mishnah, five art the books of the Torah, four art the mothers, three art the fathers, two art the tablets of the covenant, One is our God in the heavens and the earth.

Who knoweth a show of eight?[294] I knoweth eight: eight art the days of circumcision, seven art the days of the week, six art the orders of the Mishnah, five art the books of the Torah, four art the mothers, three art the fathers, two art the tablets of the covenant, One is our God in the heavens and the earth.

Who knoweth three threes for nine?[295] I knoweth nine: nine art the months due of birth,[296] eight art the days of circumcision, seven art the days of the week, six art the orders of the Mishnah, five art the books of the Torah, four art the mothers, three art the fathers, two art the tablets of the covenant, One is our God in the heavens and the earth.

Who knoweth the stroke of ten?[297] I knoweth ten: ten art the statements, nine art the months of birth, eight art the days of circumcision, seven art the days of the week, six art the orders of the Mishnah, five art the books of the Torah, four art the mothers, three art the fathers, two art the tablets of the covenant, One is our God in the heavens and the earth.

293 *Macbeth*, Act 4, Scene 1.
294 *Ibid.*
295 *Love's Labour's Lost*, Act 5, Scene 2.
296 *Troilus and Cressida*, Act 1, Scene 3.
297 *Richard III*, Act 4, Scene 2.

אַחַד עָשָׂר מִי יוֹדֵעַ? אַחַד עָשָׂר אֲנִי יוֹדֵעַ: אַחַד
עָשָׂר כּוֹכְבַיָּא, עֲשָׂרָה דִבְּרַיָּא, תִּשְׁעָה יַרְחֵי לֵדָה,
שְׁמוֹנָה יְמֵי מִילָה, שִׁבְעָה יְמֵי שַׁבַּתָּא, שִׁשָּׁה סִדְרֵי
מִשְׁנָה, חֲמִשָּׁה חוּמְשֵׁי תוֹרָה, אַרְבַּע אִמָּהוֹת,
שְׁלֹשָׁה אָבוֹת, שְׁנֵי לֻחוֹת הַבְּרִית, אֶחָד אֱלֹהֵינוּ
שֶׁבַּשָּׁמַיִם וּבָאָרֶץ.

שְׁנֵים עָשָׂר מִי יוֹדֵעַ? שְׁנֵים עָשָׂר אֲנִי יוֹדֵעַ: שְׁנֵים
עָשָׂר שִׁבְטַיָּא, אַחַד עָשָׂר כּוֹכְבַיָּא, עֲשָׂרָה דִבְּרַיָּא,
תִּשְׁעָה יַרְחֵי לֵדָה, שְׁמוֹנָה יְמֵי מִילָה, שִׁבְעָה יְמֵי
שַׁבַּתָּא, שִׁשָּׁה סִדְרֵי מִשְׁנָה, חֲמִשָּׁה חוּמְשֵׁי תוֹרָה,
אַרְבַּע אִמָּהוֹת, שְׁלֹשָׁה אָבוֹת, שְׁנֵי לֻחוֹת הַבְּרִית,
אֶחָד אֱלֹהֵינוּ שֶׁבַּשָּׁמַיִם וּבָאָרֶץ.

שְׁלֹשָׁה עָשָׂר מִי יוֹדֵעַ? שְׁלֹשָׁה עָשָׂר אֲנִי יוֹדֵעַ:
שְׁלֹשָׁה עָשָׂר מִדַּיָּא. שְׁנֵים עָשָׂר שִׁבְטַיָּא, אַחַד
עָשָׂר כּוֹכְבַיָּא, עֲשָׂרָה דִבְּרַיָּא, תִּשְׁעָה יַרְחֵי לֵדָה,
שְׁמוֹנָה יְמֵי מִילָה, שִׁבְעָה יְמֵי שַׁבַּתָּא, שִׁשָּׁה סִדְרֵי
מִשְׁנָה, חֲמִשָּׁה חוּמְשֵׁי תוֹרָה, אַרְבַּע אִמָּהוֹת,
שְׁלֹשָׁה אָבוֹת, שְׁנֵי לֻחוֹת הַבְּרִית, אֶחָד אֱלֹהֵינוּ
שֶׁבַּשָּׁמַיִם וּבָאָרֶץ.

[הָאִשָּׁה יוֹצֵאת.]

Who knoweth eleven, sir?[298] I knoweth eleven: eleven art the stars above us,[299] ten art the statements, nine art the months of birth, eight art the days of circumcision, seven art the days of the week, six art the orders of the Mishnah, five art the books of the Torah, four art the mothers, three art the fathers, two art the tablets of the covenant, One is our God in the heavens and the earth.

Who knoweth of this present twelve?[300] I knoweth twelve: twelve art the tribes, eleven art the stars, ten art the statements, nine art the months of birth, eight art the days of circumcision, seven art the days of the week, six art the orders of the Mishnah, five art the books of the Torah, four art the mothers, three art the fathers, two art the tablets of the covenant, One is our God in the heavens and the earth.

Who knoweth what had numbered thirteen[301]? I knoweth thirteen: thirteen art the characteristics, twelve art the tribes, eleven art the stars, ten art the statements, nine art the months of birth, eight art the days of circumcision, seven art the days of the week, six art the orders of the Mishnah, five art the books of the Torah, four art the mothers, three art the fathers, two art the tablets of the covenant, One is our God in the heavens and the earth.

[The wife exits.]

---

298 *Measure for Measure*, Act 2, Scene 1.
299 *King Lear*, Act 4, Scene 3.
300 *Henry IV*, Part I, Act 2, Scene 4.
301 *Twelfth Night*, Act 5, Scene 1.

חַד גַּדְיָא

[הבעל מרים את מבטו. נראה שכולם נעלמו. הוא שר לעצמו, בתשוקה.]

חַד גַּדְיָא, חַד גַּדְיָא דְזַבִּין אַבָּא בִּתְרֵי זוּזֵי, חַד
גַּדְיָא, חַד גַּדְיָא.

וְאָתָא שׁוּנְרָא וְאָכְלָה לְגַדְיָא, דְזַבִּין אַבָּא בִּתְרֵי
זוּזֵי. חַד גַּדְיָא, חַד גַּדְיָא.

וְאָתָא כַלְבָּא וְנָשַׁךְ לְשׁוּנְרָא, דְאָכְלָה לְגַדְיָא, דְזַבִּין
אַבָּא בִּתְרֵי זוּזֵי. חַד גַּדְיָא, חַד גַּדְיָא.

וְאָתָא חוּטְרָא וְהִכָּה לְכַלְבָּא, דְנָשַׁךְ לְשׁוּנְרָא,
דְאָכְלָה לְגַדְיָא, דְזַבִּין אַבָּא בִּתְרֵי זוּזֵי. חַד גַּדְיָא,
חַד גַּדְיָא.

וְאָתָא נוּרָא וְשָׂרַף לְחוּטְרָא, דְהִכָּה לְכַלְבָּא, דְנָשַׁךְ
לְשׁוּנְרָא, דְאָכְלָה לְגַדְיָא, דְזַבִּין אַבָּא בִּתְרֵי זוּזֵי.
חַד גַּדְיָא, חַד גַּדְיָא.

One Kid

[The husband looks up. Everyone seems to be gone. He sings to himself, with passion.]

One kid, one kid that mine father hath bought for two zuz, one kid, one kid.

Then cameth a gib cat[302] and consumed the kid that mine father hath bought for two zuz, one kid, one kid.

Then cameth a common dog[303] and bit the ramping cat,[304] that consumed the kid that mine father hath bought for two zuz, one kid, one kid.

Then cameth this stick[305] and hitteth the wild dog,[306] that bit the poor cat,[307] that consumed the kid that mine father hath bought for two zuz, one kid, one kid.

Then cameth pale fire[308] and burnt the stick fiery off indeed,[309] that hitteth the egregious dog,[310] that bit the brinded cat,[311] that consumed the kid that mine father hath bought for two zuz, one kid, one kid.

---

302 *Henry IV*, Part I, Act I, Scene 2.
303 *Henry IV*, Part II, Act I, Scene 3.
304 *Henry IV*, Part I, Act 3, Scene I.
305 *The Tempest*, Act I, Scene 2.
306 *Henry IV*, Part II, Act I, Scene 3.
307 *Macbeth*, Act I, Scene 7.
308 *Timon of Athens*, Act 4, Scene 3.
309 *Hamlet*, Act 5, Scene 2.
310 *Henry V*, Act 2, Scene I.
311 *Macbeth*, Act 4, Scene I.

וְאָתָא מַיָּא וְכָבָה לְנוּרָא, דְשָׂרַף לְחוּטְרָא, דְהִכָּה
לְכַלְבָּא, דְנָשַׁךְ לְשׁוּנְרָא, דְאָכְלָה לְגַדְיָא, דְזַבִּין
אַבָּא בִּתְרֵי זוּזֵי. חַד גַּדְיָא, חַד גַּדְיָא.

וְאָתָא תוֹרָא וְשָׁתָה לְמַיָּא, דְכָבָה לְנוּרָא, דְשָׂרַף
לְחוּטְרָא, דְהִכָּה לְכַלְבָּא, דְנָשַׁךְ לְשׁוּנְרָא, דְאָכְלָה
לְגַדְיָא, דְזַבִּין אַבָּא בִּתְרֵי זוּזֵי. חַד גַּדְיָא, חַד גַּדְיָא.

וְאָתָא הַשּׁוֹחֵט וְשָׁחַט לְתוֹרָא, דְשָׁתָה לְמַיָּא, דְכָבָה
לְנוּרָא, דְשָׂרַף לְחוּטְרָא, דְהִכָּה לְכַלְבָּא, דְנָשַׁךְ
לְשׁוּנְרָא, דְאָכְלָה לְגַדְיָא, דְזַבִּין אַבָּא בִּתְרֵי זוּזֵי.
חַד גַּדְיָא, חַד גַּדְיָא.

Then cameth roaring waters and extinguished the raging fire of fever bred,[312] that burnt the stick compared with this truncheon,[313] that hitteth the dog of war,[314] that bit the cat wringing her hands,[315] that consumed the kid that mine father hath bought for two zuz, one kid, one kid.

Then cameth a savage bull[316] and drank the water,[317] that allayed the fire,[318] that burnt the stick deep,[319] that hitteth the damned, inexecrable dog,[320] that bit the harmless necessary cat,[321] that consumed the kid that mine father hath bought for two zuz, one kid, one kid.

Then cameth the very butcher[322] and slaughtered the chafed bull,[323] that drank of the water,[324] that quenched the fire,[325] that burnt the stick misbecomingly,[326] that hitteth the mad dog,[327] that bit Fortune's cat,[328] that consumed the kid that mine father hath bought for two zuz, one kid, one kid.

312   The Comedy of Errors, Act 5, Scene 1.
313   Henry VI, Part II, Act 4, Scene 10.
314   Julius Caesar, Act 3, Scene 1.
315   The Two Gentlemen of Verona, Act 2, Scene 3.
316   Much Ado About Nothing, Act 1, Scene 1.
317   Henry VI, Part III, Act 5, Scene 4.
318   Henry VIII, Act 1, Scene 1.
319   Macbeth, Act 3, Scene 1.
320   The Merchant of Venice, Act 4, Scene 1.
321   Ibid.
322   Romeo and Juliet, Act 2, Scene 4.
323   Henry VI, Part III, Act 2, Scene 5.
324   Pericles, Act 2, Scene 1.
325   Romeo and Juliet, Act 1, Scene 1.
326   The Two Noble Kinsmen, Act 5, Scene 3.
327   The Merry Wives of Windsor, Act 4, Scene 2.
328   All's Well That Ends Well, Act 5, Scene 2.

דְּשָׁתָה לְמַיָּא, דְּכָבָה לְנוּרָא, דְּשָׂרַף לְחוּטְרָא,
דְּהִכָּה לְכַלְבָּא, דְּנָשַׁךְ לְשׁוּנְרָא, דְּאָכְלָה לְגַדְיָא,
דְּזַבִּין אַבָּא בִּתְרֵי זוּזֵי. חַד גַּדְיָא, חַד גַּדְיָא.

וְאָתָא הַקָּדוֹשׁ בָּרוּךְ הוּא וְשָׁחַט לְמַלְאַךְ הַמָּוֶת,
דְּשָׁחַט לְשׁוֹחֵט, דְּשָׁחַט לְתוֹרָא, דְּשָׁתָה לְמַיָּא,
דְּכָבָה לְנוּרָא, דְּשָׂרַף לְחוּטְרָא, דְּהִכָּה לְכַלְבָּא,
דְּנָשַׁךְ לְשׁוּנְרָא, דְּאָכְלָה לְגַדְיָא, דְּזַבִּין אַבָּא בִּתְרֵי
זוּזֵי. חַד גַּדְיָא, חַד גַּדְיָא.

[הבעל יוצא.]

Then cameth the gloomy shade of death[329] and slaughtered the butcher with an axe,[330] who slaughtered the town bull,[331] that drank all the water,[332] that blew the fire up[333], that broke a stick and cried,[334] that hitteth the unmannered dog,[335] that bit the Prince of cats,[336] that consumed the kid that mine father hath bought for two zuz, one kid, one kid.

Then cameth the Holy One, which by us shall blessed be[337] and slaughtered the cold hand of death,[338] who slaughtered of this dead butcher,[339] who slaughtered the strange bull,[340] that drank all the water,[341] that dashed the fire out,[342] that breaketh a stick,[343] that hitteth yonder dog,[344] that bit the Good King of cats,[345] that consumed the kid that mine father hath bought for two zuz, one kid, one kid.

[The husband exits.]

---

329 *Henry VI, Part I*, Act 4, Scene 5.
330 *Henry VI, Part II*, Act 3, Scene 2.
331 *Henry IV, Part II*, Act 2, Scene 2.
332 *Henry V*, Act 4, Scene 7.
333 *Antony and Cleopatra*, Act 2, Scene 6.
334 *King Lear*, Act 2, Scene 4.
335 *Richard III*, Act 1, Scene 2.
336 *Romeo and Juliet*, Act 2, Scene 4.
337 *A Midsummer Night's Dream*, Act 5, Scene 1.
338 *Henry IV, Part I*, Act 5, Scene 4.
339 *Macbeth*, Act 5, Scene 6.
340 *Much Ado About Nothing*, Act 5, Scene 4.
341 *Titus Andronicus*, Act 4, Scene 2.
342 *The Tempest*, Act 1, Scene 2.
343 *Henry VI, Part II*, Act 1, Scene 2.
344 *Richard III*, Act 1, Scene 3.
345 *Romeo and Juliet*, Act 3, Scene 1.

About the Author of All³⁴⁶

Martin hath been writing freelance for over two decades, mostly on Jewish interest topics. He is the co-creator of a popular Jewish news satire website called TheKnish. com. His work hath been published in *The Huffington Post, The Denver Post, The Washington Times,* The *Jewish Press, Country Yossi* Magazine, *Modern Magazine, The Jewish Link of N.J,* The Jewish Book Council, bangitout.com, scoogiespin.com, jewcentral.com, and israelinsider. com. His work hath eke been translated for Germany's only weekly Jewish newspaper, *The Jüdische Allgemeine.* He hath served as the beat reporter for

346 *Much Ado About Nothing,* Act 5, Scene 2.

JRunnersClub.org and as the surname columnist for jewishworldreview. com.

The Emoji Haggadah, *The Festivus Haggadah*, and *The Coronavirus Haggadah* generated much praise and media attention, and wast covered in *The Jewish Week*, *The Jewish Link of N.J*, *Jewish Vues*, Vos Iz Neias, Jewish Book Council, NorthJersey.com, *The Forward*, *Jewish Journal*, J-Wire, *Vox*, *The Jewish Press*, *The Jewish Fund*, *The Judische Allgemeine*, various blogs, eater.com, and *The New York Times*.

This is his tenth book. He'll consume it up, he loves it so.

Table Which Tracketh How Oft a Particular Play Is Quoth Herein

Good night, good night, parting is such sweet sorrow, that I shall say good night till it be morrow.[347]

347 *Romeo and Juliet*, Act 2, Scene 2.